Editor
Eric Migliaccio

Managing Editor
Ina Massler Levin, M.A.

Editor-in-Chief
Sharon Coan, M.S. Ed.

Illustrator
Sue Fullam

Cover Artist
Brenda DiAntonis

Art Coordinator
Kevin Barnes

Art Director
CJae Froshay

Imaging
Alfred Lau
Ralph Olmedo, Jr.

Product Manager
Phil Garcia

Publisher
Mary D. Smith, M.S. Ed.

Building Sentence Skills
Tools for Writing the Amazing English Sentence

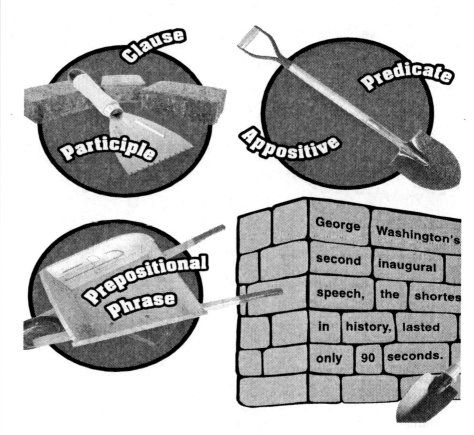

Author

Brian Backman, M.S. Ed.

Teacher Created Resources, Inc.
6421 Industry Way
Westminster, CA 92683
www.teachercreated.com
ISBN-0-7439-3704-X
©2003 Teacher Created Resources, Inc.
Reprinted, 2005
Made in U.S.A.

Table of Contents

Table of Contents (cont.)

Introduction

It is possible to teach sentence structure without numbing the minds of students. It's true that prepositional phrases, adverb clauses, and compound-complex sentences are not the most exciting teaching topics around. In fact, just mentioning these terms in class can cause students' heads to drop. However, teaching sentence structure with writing topics and activities that allow students to generate and share their own creative sentences can actually make the subject interesting and even fun.

Students will probably never be asked to identify an adverb clause or an appositive phrase during a job interview. However, the ability to write sentences that contain adverb clauses and appositive phrases will help every student get a job interview and succeed once he or she has landed the job. Writing sentences that are clear, correct, and varied is a goal for which any student should strive. Knowing the different types of phrases and clauses that writers have at their disposal is a means to that goal.

Even a great writer may not be able to identify an adverb clause or an appositive phrase, but one thing is certain: competent writers use the entire contents of the English-sentence toolbox to write sentences—and this toolbox includes adverb clauses and appositive phrases. This book will help students understand the different parts of the sentence, and it will give them new tools for expanding and revising sentences to make them more elaborate, detailed, and interesting.

Here's an overview of this book's contents:

✣ **Part I: Sentence Skills** (beginning on page 5)

Here you will find individual lessons and application writing assignments that are logically sequenced to build on each other.

✣ **Part II: Sentence Styles** (beginning on page 56)

These are lessons on specific word choice and parallelism.

✣ **Part III: Sentence Games** (beginning on page 60)

This section features classroom and small-group games in which students can apply their learning of the sentence skills.

✣ **Appendices** (beginning on page 68)

This section includes skills review, a quiz, writing assignments, and an answer key

The Amazing English Sentence

The English sentence is an amazing thing. It has a limited set of distinct parts (phrases and clauses), but these parts can be strung together and rearranged in a seemingly endless variety of ways. Furthermore, there is an incredible volume of words from which a writer can draw. Experts estimate that there are nearly 1 million words in English, and this number is growing every day. This flexibility of parts and variety in vocabulary make it possible to write a sentence that no one has ever written or even spoken before. Sure there are sentences that we hear every day, such as "I love you" or "The dog ate my homework"; but anyone using the resources of the English language can write a totally unique sentence such as, "The rabid chihuahua gobbled my potentially award-winning essay entitled '101 Alternative Uses for Ear Wax.'"

Here's an illustration that shows just how much variety is possible in the English sentence. Imagine you are writing a sentence that is 10 words long. If you had only 10 possible words to choose from for each of the 10 words in the sentence, you would have 10 billion possible different combinations of words (the formula being $10 \times 10 \times 10 \times 10 \times 10 \times 10 \times 10 \times 10 \times 10 \times 10 =$ 10 billion). If it took you 10 seconds to write a single 10-word sentence, it would take you over 3,171 years to write all 10 billion possible combinations. Try doing that for tonight's homework!

Read the following sentences, and see if you agree that they probably have never been uttered by anyone at your school.

My English teacher made us watch MTV in class today.

Yesterday, I volunteered to clean every toilet in the school.

Tomorrow, all my friends and I are going to get together and write a musical about fish sticks.

Sticks and stones may break my bones, but on Wednesday pepperoni pizza is on the school lunch menu.

The Amazing English Sentence *(cont.)*

Writing Activity

Unheard-of Sentences

Try writing your own totally unique sentences. Each sentence should be at least 10 words long, and each should be a complete sentence. Here are some tips that might help you come up with some ideas:

- Think of something that is so odd that it would never happen.
- Think of something that is so totally out of character for you (or for someone famous) that it would never happen.
- Think of an overused phrase or expression, such as "When the cat's away, the mice will play." (These are also known as clichés.) Then, rewrite the phrase so that it begins or ends in a new way, such as "When the cat's away, the mice get together and sing a medley of Elvis songs."

1. _____

   _____

   _____

2. _____

   _____

   _____

3. _____

   _____

   _____

4. _____

   _____

   _____

5. _____

   _____

   _____

Simple Sentence Sense

Which of the following is a complete sentence?

A. Book the read Sam.   **C.** The Sam read book.

B. Read book the Sam.   **D.** Sam read the book.

Even if you have never taken a class in grammar, you probably recognize that **D** is the complete sentence. You are able to recognize the correct sentence because your experience speaking, reading, and writing English sentences allows you to understand how the language works. You might say you have a sixth sense that helps you make sense of sentences. Not all sentences are as clear and as short as "Sam read the book"; however, your ability to recognize this simple sentence is an important starting point for understanding longer, more elaborate sentences.

A simple sentence is made up of two parts: a *subject* (a noun or pronoun) and a *predicate* (a verb). The subject tells who or what the sentence is about, and the predicate tells what the subject is doing or what it is. These are some examples of simple sentences:

- ➡ Jeff snores.
- ➡ My textbooks are too heavy.
- ➡ John plays the guitar while standing on his head.
- ➡ Yesterday, Joe Martin became the first person ever to bowl four straight 300 games.

Recognizing a complete sentence is not all that difficult. Use this test: imagine someone poked his head in your classroom door and said, "Today, after fourth period." You would probably be perplexed by this statement because it is not a complete thought; therefore, it does not make sense. Now imagine another person poked her head in your classroom door and said, "Today, after fourth period, all students will be given a flu shot!" This statement makes sense because it stands alone as a complete thought.

Directions: In the following sentences, underline the simple subjects (what/who the sentence is about) and circle the simple predicates (what the subject is doing or what it is). The first has been done for you.

1. <u>Ben</u> (copied) his roommate's term paper on plagiarism.

2. Magazine readers enjoy the topics of food and sports the most.

3. Arctic ground squirrels hibernate for nine months of the year.

4. The dogs ran after the paperboy.

5. In June, we plan to celebrate Donald Duck's birthday.

6. *Star Wars* is one of the highest grossing movies of all time.

7. In April, Jack never does homework.

8. The madman, tall and limping, walked silently through the night.

Bonus: Select five sentences from a book, newspaper, or magazine. Write down the five sentences and underline the subjects and circle the predicates in each of the sentences. Write down the sentence, the author, and title of the source from which you got it.

Write Your Own Simple Sentences

A simple sentence is made up of two parts: a subject (a noun or pronoun) and a predicate (a verb). The subject tells who or what the sentence is about, and the predicate tells what the subject is doing or what it is.

➥ Russ always flosses after dinner.

   Simple Subject: Russ

   Simple Predicate: flosses

➥ The quicksand swallowed my homework.

   Simple Subject: quicksand

   Simple Predicate: swallowed

➥ The state dance of Washington is the square dance.

   Simple Subject: dance

   Simple Predicate: is

Select some subjects for sentences by answering the questions below:

1. Who is a famous person you admire? _____

2. What is your favorite hobby or sport? _____

3. What is your favorite place? _____

4. What is something that annoys you? _____

Write four simple sentences by adding a predicate to each of the four subjects above. Underline each subject and circle each predicate.

1. _____

   _____

2. _____

   _____

3. _____

   _____

4. _____

   _____

Write Your Own Simple Sentences *(cont.)*

Writing Activity

Write Opening Lines to a Children's Story

Write the opening four sentences of a children's story. Introduce the main character, the setting of the story, and a problem that the character has. Think animals, magic, silliness—and simple but precise words.

Here is an example:

Rone never liked delivering the paper to Jake the Giant's house. Jake was often mean to trespassers, even trespassers who brought him his daily newspaper, *The Wartsville Chronicle*. In fact, Rone had heard rumors that Jake had eaten the last paperboy. So, as he crept quietly up the giant's walkway, Rone trembled with fear, hoping the enormous wooden door with menacing metal spikes would not open.

_____

_____

_____

_____

_____

_____

_____

_____

_____

_____

_____

_____

_____

_____

_____

_____

_____

Sentence Chemistry: Making Subjects and Predicates Compound

A simple sentence is made up of two parts: a subject (a noun or pronoun) and a predicate (a verb). The subject tells who or what the sentence is about, and the predicate tells what the subject is doing or what it is.

A subject can be a single noun, as in the following:

➡ **John** plays the guitar while standing on his head.

A subject can also be more than a single noun, as in this sentence:

➡ **John** and **Paul** play the guitar while standing on their heads.

When a subject is made up of more than a single noun, it is called a **compound subject.**

Like subjects, predicates can also be compound. Notice the difference between the following two sentences:

➡ John plays the guitar while standing on his head.

➡ John plays the guitar and reads books while standing on his head.

In the second sentence, *plays* and *reads* form a compound predicate. Both verbs share the same subject: *John.*

Directions: Read the sentences below and on page 11. Underline the subjects and circle the predicates. Also, circle the correct description below each.

1. Ben copied his roommate's term paper on plagiarism and turned it in to his ethics professor.

   compound subject   **compound predicate**

2. Magazine readers and newspaper subscribers enjoy the topics of food and sports the most.

   compound subject   **compound predicate**

3. After dinner, Jeff and Val spent the evening celebrating National Foot Care Month by cutting each other's toenails.

   compound subject   **compound predicate**

4. The dogs barked at the postman and ran after the paperboy.

   compound subject   **compound predicate**

5. In June, the freshmen and the sophomores plan to celebrate Donald Duck's birthday.

   compound subject   **compound predicate**

Sentence Chemistry: Making Subjects and Predicates Compound *(cont.)*

6. *Titanic* and *Star Wars* are the highest grossing movies of all time.

    compound subject   **compound predicate**

7. Fred sang a long song, wrote a long essay, and read a long poem after school yesterday.

    compound subject   **compound predicate**

8. In April, Jack and Ron never do homework.

    compound subject   **compound predicate**

Sentence Combining: Combine the following sentences into a single simple sentence with either a compound subject or a compound predicate:

1. Last Saturday, Ron mowed his lawn. Ron watched eight straight hours of golf. Ron rearranged his refrigerator-magnet collection.

    _____

    _____

2. The books were stacked all over the room. The magazines were stacked all over the room. The newspapers were stacked all over the room.

    _____

    _____

3. Boris woke up at 5:00 A.M. Boris jumped out of bed. Boris began doing one-arm push-ups.

    _____

    _____

Practice 1: Look over the list of 40 topics on pages 65–67. On a separate piece of paper, write at least four simple sentences with compound subjects on one or multiple topics. Then write another four simple sentences with compound predicates on one or multiple topics.

Practice 2: At random, select a noun and a verb from the lists on page 63, and combine the words by using them in a simple sentence. You may alter the noun or verb; however, you must use the noun as a noun and the verb as a verb. On a separate piece of paper, write eight simple sentences with eight different random combinations of nouns and verbs.

Bonus: Find an example of a sentence with a compound predicate either in a work of fiction you are reading or in a newspaper or magazine article/advertisement. Write down the sentence, the author, and title of the source from which you got it.

Write Your Own Sentences with Compound Predicates

The sentences below all have compound predicates. In each the subject of the sentence is doing more than one thing. Notice that the verbs are underlined.

➡ The goofy ghoul <u>grows</u> festering weeds and <u>collects</u> frog drool.
➡ The major monstrosity <u>eats</u> slimy slugs and <u>reads</u> Shakespeare.
➡ The coldhearted creature <u>writes</u> sonnets and <u>hates</u> homework.
➡ The dangerous demon <u>loves</u> housework and <u>drinks</u> pond scum.

In the table of monster descriptions below, four separate sentences are broken up into the following categories:

✗ **Subjects (A)**
✗ **Predicates (B and C)**

Any subject from any row in column A can be selected and combined with predicates from B and C to form a complete sentence. For example, the subject in row 1, column A can be combined with the predicate from row 2, column B and the predicate in row 3, column C to form this sentence: *The goofy ghoul grows festering weeds and collects frog drool.* If you were to form all the possible combinations, you would have 64 separate sentences.

Monster Combinations

Directions: Add four more subjects in column A below by coming up with different types of monsters. Then add four predicates in column B and four predicates in column C. If you complete the table correctly, you will be able to generate over 500 different possible combinations!

	A. Subject	B. Predicate	C. Predicate
Row 1	The goofy ghoul	eats slimy slugs	reads Shakespeare.
Row 2	The coldhearted creature	grows festering weeds	drinks pond scum.
Row 3	The dangerous dude	loves homework	collects frog drool.
Row 4	The major monstrosity	writes romantic poems	hates homework.
Row 5	The		
Row 6	The		
Row 7	The		
Row 8	The		

Write Your Own Sentences with Compound Predicates *(cont.)*

Using random combinations of columns A, B, and C from the chart on page 12, write five sentences with compound predicates.

1. _____

    _____

2. _____

    _____

3. _____

    _____

4. _____

    _____

5. _____

    _____

Writing Activity

Monster Description

Write a description of a monster. Use three predicates in your sentence. For example: *The hideous hag hides under beds, laughs loudly in the dark, and loves to eat small children.*

_____

_____

_____

_____

_____

_____

_____

Adjectives: the Good, the Bad, and the Ugly

What do a *good* book, a *bad* dog, and an *ugly* prom dress have in common? They all use adjectives. Adjectives are words that you can use to describe nouns. For example, if you are describing a movie that you just saw, you might say it was an action-packed, riveting, and heart-stopping movie. Here are some examples:

➡ The bossy, loud janitor ordered the students to stop eating in the hall.

➡ The hostile, boisterous, and frenzied crowd roared as the kazoo band took the stage.

➡ Last night Bill had a dream in which he went snorkeling in a large, festering vat of chicken fat.

As you can see in the examples above, adjectives can be used in combination—but notice that sometimes a comma is used between the adjectives, and sometimes one is not.

➡ We only eat pancakes now that our old waffle iron is no longer working.

➡ Mary realized that she had a stinky, disgusting job on her hands when her Aunt Thelma accidentally flushed her false teeth down the toilet.

If the adjectives can be reversed, you need a comma; if the adjectives cannot be reversed, don't use a comma. If you were to say "our waffle old iron is no longer working," the sentence would not make sense; however, whether you say a "stinky, disgusting job" or a "disgusting, stinky job" the sentence makes sense.

While adjectives are usually found in front of the noun or pronoun they describe, they may also come after the noun. Read the three sentences below and observe how the two adjectives *bossy* and *loud* are positioned differently to describe the noun *janitor*.

➡ <u>Bossy and loud,</u> the janitor ordered the students to stop eating in the hall.

➡ The janitor, <u>bossy and loud,</u> ordered the students to stop eating in the hall.

➡ The <u>bossy, loud</u> janitor ordered the students to stop eating in the hall.

Directions: Underline the adjectives in the following sentences.

1. The loud, annoying music of the ice cream truck blared through the neighborhood all summer.

2. The restless, eager students waited impatiently by the radio to find out whether or not school had been cancelled because of the snowstorm.

3. Joe bought a new electric guitar with the money he was supposed to use for accordion lessons.

4. Brett soon realized that using a high-pressure water hose was the wrong way to bathe his cat.

5. Joe was in for a shock when he went to work at the electric car wash.

6. The police were baffled by a mysterious, unexplained string of doghouse robberies.

7. George recently recorded his first CD of electric washboard music.

8. The cold, freezing rain fell throughout the night.

Adjectives: the Good, the Bad, and the Ugly *(cont.)*

Sentence Combining: Combine the following sentences into a single sentence with adjectives.

1. Their peaceful evening was interrupted. Their relaxing evening was interrupted. It was interrupted by a barrage of calls by an annoying phone solicitor.

   _____

   _____

   _____

   _____

2. Joe built a tower. The tower was 500 feet tall. The tower was built out of empty milk cartons.

   _____

   _____

   _____

   _____

3. Marsha's favorite meal is eggplant. She likes it smothered in hot maple syrup.

   _____

   _____

   _____

   _____

Practice 1: Look over the list of 40 topics on pages 65–67. On a separate piece of paper, write at least eight sentences with adjectives on one or multiple topics

Practice 2: At random, select a noun and a verb from the lists on page 63, and combine the words by using them in a sentence with adjectives. You may alter the noun or verb; however, you must use the noun as a noun and the verb as a verb. On a separate piece of paper, write eight simple sentences with eight different random combinations of nouns and verbs.

Bonus: Find an example of a sentence with at least two adjectives either in a work of fiction you are reading or in a newspaper or magazine article/ad. Write down the sentence, the author, and title of the source from which you got it. Also, underline the adjectives.

Write Your Own Sentences with Adjectives

What do the following sentences have in common?

➥ The quiet, stealthy alley cat crept up on the mouse.

➥ The eager, energized student started his homework early.

➥ Opening their thick history textbooks to read, the students smiled in anticipation.

They all use adjectives to describe nouns.

It is not hard to include adjectives in your own writing. Look at the step-by-step instructions box below.

Step by Step: How to Write a Sentence with Adjectives

Step 1: Write a simple sentence, and determine what nouns you will use in your sentence.

The dog bit the paper carrier.

Step 2: Generate adjectives that you might use to describe the nouns. Use the word *very* to help you generate possible descriptive words.

Dog Description (*very*): vicious, ferocious, rabid, flea-bitten, unchained

Paper Carrier Description (*very*): inexperienced, frightened, fleeing, terrified

Step 3: Expand the sentence with the adjectives.

The vicious, flea-bitten dog bit the frightened, fleeing paper carrier.

Write Your Own Sentences
with Adjectives *(cont.)*

**Writing
Activity**

Restaurant Review

Follow the instructions in the step-by-step box to write your own sentences with adjectives. On the lines below write five sentences reviewing a restaurant in your hometown, and underline all adjectives. Describe the sights, sounds, smells, and tastes of the place.

Here is an example:

When you walk into Joe's Grill, you are overwhelmed by the fragrant smells of frying burgers; the warm, comfortable welcome of the attentive wait staff; and the hip, colorful décor of this fine restaurant's interior.

_____

_____

_____

_____

_____

_____

_____

_____

How I Learned to Stop Worrying and Love the Adverb

The sentences below all tell how a shopper maneuvered a shopping cart through a grocery store. In each sentence the underlined words are adverbs. Adverbs modify verbs by telling how the action is done. Adverbs frequently end in **ly**.

➡ The angry shopper aggressively steered his shopping cart through the cold cereal aisle.

➡ Steering his shopping cart skillfully through the cold cereal aisle, the shopper was looking for prune juice.

➡ Quickly, the angry shopper steered his shopping cart through the cold cereal aisle.

➡ Swiftly and forcefully, the angry shopper steered his shopping cart through the cold cereal aisle.

Adverbs may be used at the beginning of a sentence as an opening, before a verb, or after a verb. The chart below offers an example of each. As you draft, revise, and edit, experiment with the most effective positioning.

Sentence Opening	Enthusiastically and proudly, the dentist announced that he had invented a cavity-fighting candy bar.
Before a Verb	The dentist enthusiastically and proudly announced that he had invented a cavity-fighting candy bar.
After a Verb	The dentist announced enthusiastically and proudly that he had invented a cavity-fighting candy bar.

Directions: In the following sentences, underline any adverbs that answer "how."

1. The Easter egg hunt was cancelled after several parents greedily rushed past the children to grab the colored eggs.

2. Graceful and sensuous, Geneva walked across the hot bed of coals.

3. The young boy guiltily returned the overdue library book entitled *How to Overcome Procrastination.*

4. Mary politely helped Jim to see the obvious problem with his idea of creating a chain of all-you-can-eat to-go restaurants.

5. Lem sweated profusely as he repaired the leaky toilet.

6. Ron quietly asked the waiter for a doggy bag.

7. Paul's mother told him loudly and clearly to keep the toilet seat down.

8. Carlos walked gingerly through the hot bed of coals.

How I Learned to Stop Worrying and Love the Adverb *(cont.)*

Sentence Combining: Combine the following sentences into a single sentence with adverbs.

1. Mary's head swayed as she listened to her favorite CD. Her head swayed rhythmically.

_____

_____

_____

_____

2. Bill opened his letter from the Long Ranger Fan Club. Bill opened his letter anxiously.

_____

_____

_____

_____

3. Nancy slipped her overdue library books into the return slot. She slipped them in quickly. She slipped them in quietly.

_____

_____

_____

_____

Practice 1: Look over the list of 40 topics on pages 65–67. On a separate piece of paper, write at least eight simple sentences with adverbs on one or multiple topics

Practice 2: At random, select a noun and a verb from the lists on page 63, and combine the words by using them in a sentence with adverbs. You may alter the noun or verb; however, you must use the noun as a noun and the verb as a verb. On a separate piece of paper, write eight simple sentences with eight different random combinations of nouns and verbs.

Bonus: Find an example of a sentence that uses adverbs either in a work of fiction you are reading or in a newspaper or magazine article/ad. On a separate piece of paper, write down the sentence and the author and title of the source form which you got it. Also, underline the adverbs.

Write Your Own Sentences with Adverbs

There are many ways to expand a sentence to give the reader more information. One of the most important ways to do this is to use adverbs. Adverbs modify verbs by telling how something is done.

Notice how the sentences below are expanded by using adverbs:

Original Sentence	Revised Sentence
While playing Monopoly, Bill demanded to be the car instead of the thimble.	While playing Monopoly, Bill calmly and quietly demanded to be the car instead of the thimble.

The revised sentence tells how Bill demanded.

Original Sentence	Revised Sentence
The football team fought to defeat the cheerleaders in tug-of-war.	The football team fought tirelessly and tenaciously to defeat the cheerleaders in tug-of-war.

The revised sentence tells how the team fought.

Original Sentence	Revised Sentence
The rain fell on the small town.	The rain fell relentlessly on the small town.

The revised sentence tells how the rain fell.

Write Your Own Sentences with Adverbs *(cont.)*

It is not hard to include adverbs in your own writing. Look at the step-by-step instructions box below.

Step by Step: How to Write a Sentence with Adverbs

Step 1: Write a simple sentence:

Bill inventoried his rubber band collection.

Step 2: Identify the verbs in your sentence and generate some adverbs that tell how that action might be done.

How?: carefully, meticulously, happily, eagerly, excitedly

Step 3: Revise your sentence by expanding it with adverbs.

Meticulously, Bill inventoried his rubber band collection.

or

Bill carefully inventoried his rubber band collection.

Writing Activity

Crime, Detective, or Mystery Novel

Follow the instructions in the step-by-step box to write sentences with adverbs. Write three sentences that might be in a crime, detective, or mystery story. Underline the adverbs in your sentences. Think about who your main character is, what he/she is doing, and how he/she is doing it. Think bank robbery, fingerprints, and car chases.

Here is an example:

Gary calmly and tearfully explained to the private detective how he managed to accidentally leave his wife at a rest area in Braxton, Mississippi.

1. _____

   _____

2. _____

   _____

3. _____

   _____

Prepositional Phrases: Above and Beyond the Call of Duty

Preposition is a long name for a type of word that is usually very short. For example, words like *of, as, at, on, by, off, for, into,* and *over* are all prepositions. These little words may be small, but they are the workhorses of our language, allowing us to expand our sentences by telling more about both the nouns and verbs in our sentences.

Suppose, for example, that you were trying to describe something that you saw in the cafeteria at lunch. Without prepositions you could say:

➡ The dim-witted 7th grader threw a tater-tot.

With prepositions, however, look at how much more you can say in a single sentence (prepositions are in bold):

➡ **In** the cafeteria **at** the end of lunch, the dim-witted 7th grader **with** scrawny arms and a smirk **on** his face threw a tater-tot **at** the vice principal.

Notice that at the end of each phrase that begins with a preposition you will find a noun or a pronoun. Prepositional phrases always begin with a preposition and end with a noun or pronoun (for example, *in the cafeteria, at the end, of lunch, with scrawny arms, on his face,* and *at the vice principal*).

◆◆◆Prepositions◆◆◆

• about	• among	• beyond	• in	• past	• underneath
• at	• before	• by	• into	• since	• until
• above	• behind	• down	• like	• through	• up
• across	• below	• during	• of	• throughout	• upon
• after	• beneath	• except	• off	• to	• with
• against	• beside	• for	• on	• toward	• within
• along	• between	• from	• over	• under	• without

Prepositional phrases appear at the opening of sentences, in the middle of sentences, and at the closing of sentences.

Opening	In the cafeteria, students gathered to watch the multimedia dental hygiene demonstration.
Middle	Students gathered in the cafeteria to watch the multimedia dental hygiene demonstration.
Closing	Students gathered to watch the multimedia dental hygiene demonstration in the cafeteria.

One sentence may contain many prepositional phrases, and often prepositional phrases are used consecutively. Here is an example:

In the cafeteria at 11:00 A.M., students gathered to watch the multimedia dental hygiene demonstration.

Prepositional Phrases: Above and Beyond the Call of Duty *(cont.)*

Directions: In the sentences below, circle all prepositions and underline all prepositional phrases:

1. In his sweaty bowling shoes, Josh ran a record mile.

2. Ron sings so loudly in his shower that the neighbors frequently gather on his lawn to play "Name That Tune."

3. The small boy with big blue eyes made a $10,000 deposit into his bank account.

4. The teacher announced in a loud, raspy voice that he did not accept late work.

5. The child learned to read before his first birthday.

6. The local police announced that they have found a 10-foot crocodile in the city sewer system.

7. Over the mountain and through the forest, the family traveled for five hours before they stopped to ask for directions.

8. Crawling in a dirty T-shirt, the boy found the hidden money under the house.

Sentence Combining: Combine the following sentences into a single sentence with at least one prepositional phrase.

1. Susan swam. She swam in her neon pink swimsuit. She swam towards the shore.

   _____

   _____

2. The books were out-of-date encyclopedias. The books were on the library bookshelf.

   _____

   _____

3. Bill kept his prize-winning photographs. His photographs were of mailboxes. He kept them in a leather-bound photo album.

   _____

   _____

Practice 1: Look over the list of 40 topics on pages 65–67. On a separate piece of paper, write at least eight sentences with prepositional phrases on one or multiple topics

Practice 2: At random, select a noun and a verb from the lists on page 63, and combine the words by using them in a sentence with at least one prepositional phrase. You may alter the noun or verb; however, you must use the noun as a noun and the verb as a verb. On a separate piece of paper, write eight simple sentences with eight different random combinations of nouns and verbs.

Bonus: Find an example of a sentence that uses prepositional phrases. Choose your sentence from either a work of fiction or a newspaper or magazine article/ad. On a separate piece of paper, write the sentence and the author and title of the source from which you got it. Underline the prepositional phrases.

Write Your Own Sentences with Prepositional Phrases

What do all of these sentences have in common?

➡ Behind the bowling alley, he found a red, high-heeled bowling shoe with pink shoelaces.

➡ The story problems in my math textbook always make me cry.

➡ Fifty-six percent of men claim that they love to cook.

Each of these sentences contains at least one prepositional phrase. Prepositional phrases consist of a preposition and a noun or pronoun. They give the reader more information about the subject and/or the verb, such as the time of the action, the location, or other relationships. Prepositional phrases always begin with a preposition and end with a noun.

Prepositional Phrases

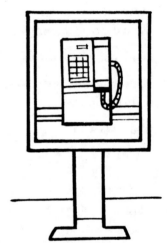

- after brunch
- since June
- into thin air
- by presidential order

- before the wrestling match
- behind the outhouse
- over the mountain
- inside the phone booth

Example Sentences

➡ *In the laboratory*, the scientist prepared a tuna sandwich.

➡ The new bakery features croissants stuffed *with bubble gum*.

It is not hard to include prepositional phrases in your own writing. Look at the step-by-step instructions box below.

Step by Step: How to Write a Sentence with a Prepositional Phrase

Step 1: Write a simple sentence:

Josh ran a record mile.

Step 2: Think of prepositional phrases that you might use to give the reader more information:

- after lunch
- with a full stomach of macaroni and cheese
- in his bowling shoes

Step 3: Expand the sentence with the prepositional phrases:

After lunch, Josh, with a stomach full of macaroni and cheese, ran a record mile in his bowling shoes.

Write Your Own Sentences with Prepositional Phrases *(cont.)*

Writing Activity

News Event at Your School or Town

Follow the instructions in the step-by-step box to write your own sentences with prepositional phrases. On the lines below, write three sentences that create and describe three separate events that would make news if they happened at your school. Underline all prepositional phrases. Make sure to answer the questions *who*, *what*, *when*, and *where* in your story.

Here is an example:

Yesterday in the faculty lounge the principal announced in a loud voice that teachers must not assign homework over the weekend.

1. _____

_____

_____

_____

_____

2. _____

_____

_____

_____

_____

3. _____

_____

_____

_____

_____

Accentuate the Appositive

You may think that only grammar teachers and the editors of the *New York Times* use *appositives*. Appositive is a fancy sounding word for something you probably do every day. Look at the sentences below. They each use an appositive.

➡ Mary, a creative cook, prepared her secret energy drink by placing a two-pound block of Spam into the blender and pouring in a gallon of buttermilk.

➡ Jennifer, the girl from second period with red hair, thinks you are cute.

➡ Mom, please let me watch *The Simpsons*, my favorite show in the entire world, before I start my homework.

If you ever use sentences like these, you use appositives. Appositives are phrases that rename a nearby noun or explain it more fully. Appositives usually interrupt a sentence.

Here is a sentence without an appositive:

➡ It gets so cold in International Falls, Minnesota, that they hold an annual frozen-turkey bowling tournament.

Here is the same sentence with an appositive that tells more about International Falls:

➡ It gets so cold in International Falls, Minnesota, a town near the Canadian border, that they hold an annual frozen-turkey bowling tournament.

Directions: Underline the appositives in the following sentences. Circle the noun that the appositive relates to.

1. Talking for hours about their lint collections, the two men, old friends, forgot to eat dinner.

2. Ron Smith, the world's most honest police officer, arrested his own mother for jaywalking.

3. A library book that was checked out in 1823 was returned in 1968, 145 years later, by the borrower's great-grandson.

4. The song, an old Scottish waltz, was not a popular choice at the senior prom.

5. George Washington's second inaugural speech, the shortest in history, lasted only 90 seconds.

6. Cathy sat whispering softly to her cat, a large tabby.

7. Joy, an avid photographer, filled her scrapbook with photos of her neighbors' mailboxes.

8. After every race he wins, Ron, a miler on our high school track team, takes off his shoe, fills it with Gatorade, and guzzles down the contents.

Accentuate the Appositive *(cont.)*

Sentence Combining: Combine the following sentences into a single simple sentence.

1. Felix took his two most valuable possessions with him on his vacation. He took his baseball cards and his pet slug.

   _____

   _____

   _____

   _____

2. Callie wants to teach her dummy how to speak French. Callie is an amateur ventriloquist.

   _____

   _____

   _____

   _____

3. Joe sat quietly. He sat eating his favorite meal. His favorite meal is a cottage cheese and Spam sandwich.

   _____

   _____

   _____

   _____

Practice 1: Look over the list of 40 topics on pages 65–67. On a separate piece of paper, write at least eight simple sentences with appositive phrases on one or multiple topics.

Practice 2: At random, select a noun and a verb from the lists on page 63, and combine the words by using them in a sentence with an appositive phrase. You may alter the noun or verb; however, you must use the noun as a noun and the verb as a verb. On a separate piece of paper, write eight simple sentences with eight different random combinations of nouns and verbs.

Bonus: Find an example of a sentence that uses an appositive from a book, newspaper or magazine article. Write the sentence and underline the appositive. Write the author and the title of the source from which you got it.

Write Your Own Sentences with Appositive Phrases

What do all of these sentences have in common?

➡ *Joe, the best writer in his class, is an outstanding juggler.*

➡ *Babe Ruth, the New York Yankees slugger, earned $50,000 in 1923.*

➡ *A chicken of the woods mushroom, the world's heaviest edible fungus, grew to weigh 100 pounds.*

Each of these sentences contains an appositive phrase. An appositive phrase is a phrase that renames a nearby noun or explains it more fully.

It is not hard to include appositive phrases in your own writing. Look at the step-by-step instructions box below.

Step by Step: How to Write a Sentence with an Appositive Phrase

Step 1: Write a sentence:

William Taft was the first president to own a car.

Step 2: Identify at least one noun in your sentence, and rename it:

William Taft: the 22nd president of the United States

Step 3: Revise your sentence adding the appositives.

William Taft, the 22nd president of the United States, was the first president to own a car.

Write Your Own Sentences with Appositive Phrases *(cont.)*

Writing Activity

Promotional Ad for Your State or Hometown

Follow the instructions in the step-by-step box to write your own sentences with appositive phrases. Write three sentences that might be used in a promotional advertisement promoting tourism in your state or hometown.

Here is an example:

Located in Washington on Puget Sound, Anacortes, gateway to the San Juan Islands, is the ideal destination for tulip lovers, whale watchers, and boat owners.

1. _____

   _____

   _____

2. _____

   _____

   _____

3. _____

   _____

   _____

There's a Party in Every Participle

When you think of participial phrases, think of a masquerade party. Participial phrases are "dressed up" like verbs, but they function as adjectives to describe nouns. Like any good party-goer, a participial phrase injects more action into a sentence. For example, the sentence below has no participial phrase:

➡ The baseball fan attempted to get the peanut man's attention.

Now, notice how we can add a participial phrase that describes the baseball fan, and notice how the participial injects more action into the sentence:

➡ Screaming loudly, the baseball fan attempted to get the peanut man's attention.

The participial phrase *screaming loudly* describes the baseball fan and tells us what he/she is doing.

Participial phrases are either in the present tense or the past tense. Here's an example of a past participial:

➡ Having screamed the entire game, the baseball fan lost his voice.

Here are more examples of sentences with participial phrases:

➡ Thinking about the homework he didn't do last night, Bill walked to school.
➡ The children, covered in dirt, returned from building their underground fortress.
➡ The students, wishing that school would last just one more week, reluctantly went home for summer vacation.
➡ Hannah looked over the salad bar, hoping it had bacon bits.

Directions: Underline any participial phrases in the following sentences:

1. Reading a magazine article on effective flossing techniques, Bill waited for his dentist appointment.

2. Joe, laughing at the joke, almost choked on his pizza.

3. Eating a banana, the gorilla looked outside its cage; eating an ice-cream cone, the boy looked inside the cage.

4. Guzzling a half-gallon of past-date 2% milk in 60 seconds, Ronald won the bet and collected $5.

5. Martha worked three hours overtime, repairing the chili pump at the corner convenience store.

6. Using a separate car key for each of his ears, Ed removed an above average amount of ear wax.

7. Spending at least four hours brainstorming, Pam generated 500 alternative uses for a paper clip.

8. Removing a large glob of gum from his mouth, the indecisive freshman couldn't decide whether to deposit it behind his ear or under his desk.

9. Taking copious notes on the differences between males and females, Jerry was fascinated to learn that men burp on average 4.7 times a day while women burp on average 2.1 times a day.

There's a Party in Every Participle *(cont.)*

Sentence Combining: Combine the following sentences into a single sentence with at least one participial phrase.

1. Gary was hoping to find his missing sweat sock. He plunged his arm into the dirty-clothes hamper.

   _____

   _____

   _____

   _____

2. Linda sang every Beatles song she knew. She tried to entertain her guests from England.

   _____

   _____

   _____

   _____

3. The woman was talking in a loud, raspy voice. The woman annoyed everyone by giving away the movie's ending.

   _____

   _____

   _____

   _____

Practice 1: Look over the list of 40 topics on pages 65–67. On a separate piece of paper, write at least eight sentences with participial phrases on one or multiple topics.

Practice 2: At random, select a noun and a verb from the lists on page 63, and combine the words by using them in a sentence with participial phrases. You may alter the noun or verb; however, you must use the noun as a noun and the verb as a verb. On a separate piece of paper, write eight simple sentences with eight different random combinations of nouns and verbs.

Bonus: Find an example of a sentence that uses participial phrases either in a work of fiction you are reading or in a newspaper or magazine article/ad. On a separate piece of paper, write down the sentence and the author and title of the source from which you got it. Underline the participial phrases.

Write Your Own Sentences with Participial Phrases

What do the following sentences have in common?

➡ Larry, singing loudly in the shower, forgot the words to "Dancing Queen."

➡ Smiling and humming a happy tune, Mary completed her geometry homework.

➡ Embarrassed to be seen wearing his Batman pajamas, the high school sophomore never answered the door in the morning.

➡ Joy went to bed, angry that she had lost her famous recipe for chicken backs and rice.

Participial phrases are verbs that work like adjectives to describe nouns. In the above sentences, "singing loudly in the shower" describes Larry; "Smiling and humming a happy tune" describes Mary; "Embarrassed to be seen wearing his Batman pajamas" describes the high school sophomore; and "angry that she had lost her famous recipe for chicken backs and rice" describes Joy.

It is not hard to include participial phrases in your own writing. Look at the step-by-step instructions box below.

Step by Step: How to Write a Sentence with a Participial Phrase

Step 1: Write a sentence about a subject using the helping verb *was* or is followed by an *-ing* verb:

The vice president was smiling.

Step 2: Eliminate the helping verb *was* or *is* and move the *-ing* verb in front of the noun so that it becomes a participle modifying the noun:

Smiling, the vice president

Step 3: Add a predicate and other details to complete the sentence:

Smiling, the vice president handed the president his birthday present, a toilet paper dispenser that played "Hail to the Chief."

Write Your Own Sentences with Participial Phrases *(cont.)*

Characters in Conflict

Writing Activity

Follow the instructions in the step-by-step box to write your own sentences with participial phrases. Write opening lines to three separate adventure stories that open with the main character in immediate conflict. Use participial phrases (underline each one) to give the reader a sense of coming into the story in the middle of the action.

1. Open the short story with a line in which the main character is in conflict with himself or herself about a decision that must be made. The following is an example:

   Grimacing as he approached the Dairy Queen drive-up window, Secret Agent Gill could never remember how to order his strawberry milkshake: was it "shaken, not stirred" or "stirred, but not shaken"?

   _____

   _____

   _____

   _____

2. Open the short story with a line in which the main character is in conflict with an antagonist. The following is an example:

   Smiling at the thought of revenging his defeat to his archenemy Jason "Banana Cream" Bailey, Chris entered the pie-eating contest.

   _____

   _____

   _____

   _____

3. Open the short story with a line in which the main character is in conflict with nature.

   Struggling against the strong currents of the river, Eric used every ounce of his energy to swim to the far shore.

   _____

   _____

   _____

   _____

Time Is Money, Knowledge Is Power, and Predicate Nouns Are an Easy Equation

There is a special kind of sentence that you probably use every day. It is the kind of sentence in which you say one thing is something else, such as:

➥ Knowledge is power.

➥ Time is money.

➥ I was a teenage Frankenstein.

➥ The new captain of the origami team will be Stephanie.

In these sentences a noun or pronoun is linked to another noun that renames, identifies, or explains the subject. This type of sentence contains a **predicate noun**, and the verb that links the two nouns is appropriately called a **linking verb**. Every predicate noun has a linking verb. Most of the time (but not always) the linking verb is some form of the verb *to be*.

Linking Verbs

Forms of *to be*	Other linking verbs
• am • is • are • was • were • be • will be • being • been	• appear • become • feel • grow • look • remain • seem • smell • sound • taste

Time Is Money, Knowledge Is Power, and Predicate Nouns Are an Easy Equation *(cont.)*

Directions: Label the sentences below that contain predicate nouns with the initials **PN**, and circle the linking verb. Label the sentences that are not predicate nouns with an **X**.

_____ 1. In Nebraska, football is a religion.

_____ 2. Hannah's driving teacher is a taskmaster.

_____ 3. Green ketchup is tasty.

_____ 4. High school water polo will be the sport of the 21st century.

_____ 5. The large curd cottage cheese is turning green and moldy.

_____ 6. No man is an island.

_____ 7. Our high schools are public institutions of learning.

_____ 8. The first casualty of war is the truth.

Practice 1: Look over the list of 40 topics on pages 65–67. On a separate piece of paper, write at least eight sentences with predicate nouns on one or multiple topics

Practice 2: At random, select a noun and a verb from the lists on page 63, and combine the words by using them in a sentence with a predicate noun. You may alter the noun or verb; however, you must use the noun as a noun and the verb as a verb. On a separate piece of paper, write eight simple sentences with eight different random combinations of nouns and verbs.

Bonus: Find an example of a sentence that uses a predicate noun either in a work of fiction you are reading or in a newspaper or magazine article/ad. On a separate piece of paper, write down the sentence and the author and title of the source from which you got it. Underline the predicate noun.

Write Your Own Sentences with Predicate Nouns

What do the following sentences have in common?

➡ Psychedelic Mouse Pad is the name of Scott's new band.

➡ Ron's favorite meal used to be alphabet soup.

➡ A psychedelic mouse pad is a necessity for every computer user.

➡ I am a rock.

➡ Failure is not an option.

In a sentence with a predicate noun, a noun or pronoun is linked to another noun that renames, identifies, or explains the subject. The verb that links the two nouns is appropriately called a linking verb. Every predicate noun has a linking verb.

It is not hard to include predicate nouns in your own writing. Look at the step-by-step instructions box below.

Step by Step: How to Write a Sentence with a Predicate Noun

Step 1: Pick a subject: Money

Step 2: Pick some nouns that rename the subject.

   Rename: a necessary evil, the root of all evil, a tool, a priority

Step 3: Add a form of the linking verb *to be* (or other linking verb) to link the subject with the renaming word:

   Linking Verbs: (Forms of *to be*): am, is, are, was, were, be, will be, being, been

   (Other linking verbs): appear, become, feel, grow, look, remain, seem, smell, sound, taste

Sentence with Predicate Noun: Money is a necessary evil.

Write Your Own Sentences with Predicate Nouns *(cont.)*

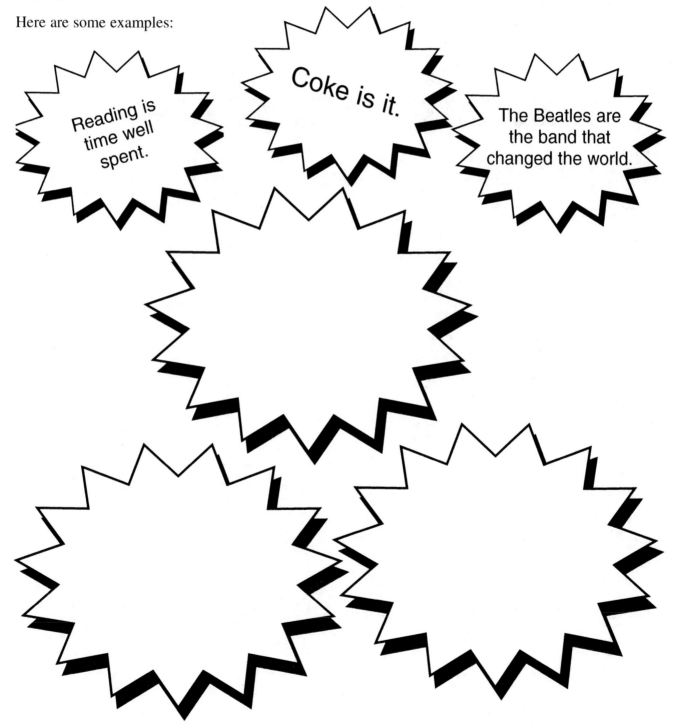

Slogan for a Product or Public Service

Follow the instructions in the step-by-step box to write your own sentences with predicate nouns. Write three new public service announcements or new promotional slogans for three different products or activities.

Here are some examples:

Reading is time well spent.

Coke is it.

The Beatles are the band that changed the world.

Roses Are Red, Violets Are Blue, Predicate Adjectives Are Nothing New

Every day we ask people to describe how they are feeling, saying "How are you?" The reply they give, such as "I'm fine" or "I'm a little sick today," is a special kind of sentence that has a **predicate adjective.**

With a predicate adjective, the subject of a sentence is linked with an adjective that describes the subject. The verb that links the subject and the adjective is appropriately called a linking verb. Every predicate adjective has a linking verb. Most of the time (but not always) the linking verb is some form of the verb *to be*.

Linking Verbs

Forms of *to be*	Other linking verbs
• am • is • are • was • were • be • will be • being • been	• appear • become • feel • grow • look • remain • seem • smell • sound • taste

Here are some examples of predicate adjectives:

➡ Roses are red.

➡ Although he was having a bad hair day, Einstein was happy.

➡ Infanticide is rampant among prairie dogs.

➡ The students looked confused.

Roses Are Red, Violets Are Blue, Predicate Adjectives Are Nothing New *(cont.)*

Directions: Label the sentences below that contain predicate adjectives with the initials **PA** and circle the linking verb. Label the sentences that are not predicate adjectives with an **X**.

_____ 1. Love is blind.

_____ 2. The students were eager to see their report cards.

_____ 3. The mouse pad is psychedelic.

_____ 4. Henry is ecstatic because he is finally going to Florida to visit the Tupperware Museum Gallery of Historical Food Containers.

_____ 5. Alphabet soup is the type of soup that librarians like the best.

_____ 6. In Nebraska, the winters are never-ending.

_____ 7. Life is not fair.

_____ 8. Russ is eating a ham sandwich.

Practice 1: Look over the list of 40 topics on pages 65–67. On a separate piece of paper, write at least eight sentences with a predicate adjective on one or multiple topics.

Practice 2: At random, select a noun and a verb from the lists on page 63, and combine the words by using them in a sentence with a predicate adjective. You may alter the noun or verb; however, you must use the noun as a noun and the verb as a verb. On a separate piece of paper, write eight simple sentences with eight different random combinations of nouns and verbs.

Bonus: Find an example of a sentence that uses a predicate adjective either in a work of fiction you are reading or in a newspaper or magazine article/ad. On a separate piece of paper, write down the sentence and the author and title of the source from which you got it. Underline the predicate adjective.

Write Your Own Sentences with Predicate Adjectives

What do the following sentences have in common?

➥ Violets are blue.

➥ My feet are huge.

➥ Because his underarm deodorant is prune-scented, Gary is angry.

➥ The new solar-powered laptop computers were expensive.

They all contain predicate adjectives. In a predicate adjective the subject of a sentence is linked with an adjective that describes the subject. The verb that links the subject and the adjective is appropriately called a linking verb. Every predicate adjective has a linking verb. Most of the time (but not always) the linking verb is some form of the verb *to be*.

It is not hard to include predicate adjectives in your own writing. Look at the step-by-step instructions box below.

Step by Step: How to Write a Sentence with a Predicate Adjective

Step 1: Pick a subject: Chess

Step 2: Pick some adjectives that describe the subject:

   Adjectives: strenuous, logical, exhausting, taxing

Step 3: Add a form of the linking verb to be (or other linking verb) to link the subject with the adjective:

   Linking Verbs: (Forms of *to be*): am, is, are, was, were, be, will be, being, been

   (Other linking verbs): appear, become, feel, grow, look, remain, seem, smell, sound, taste

Sentence with Predicate Adjective: Chess is strenuous.

Write Your Own Sentences with Predicate Adjectives *(cont.)*

Writing Activity

Dream Vacation Postcard

Follow the instructions in the step-by-step box to write your own sentences with predicate adjectives. Write five sentences that you might include on a postcard from your dream vacation. Make your readers wish they were there by describing the different places and sights you see.

For example, here's a postcard from Seattle:

The Space Needle is enormous and scenic.

Pike Place Market is so amazing that we went back

five times. The weather is awful, but the sunsets are beautiful.

The service at the restaurants has been impeccable. And although I

normally don't like fish, the salmon I had for dinner last night

was delicious.

Complex Sentences Made Easy

A complex sentence is a sentence in which at least two ideas are combined into a single sentence. What's so "complex" about that? For example, look at the following sentence:

➡ Because he forgot his wedding anniversary for the tenth straight year, Roger spent a week sleeping on the porch.

The two ideas expressed in the sentence are:

1. Roger forgot his wedding anniversary for the tenth straight year, *and*
2. Roger spent a week sleeping on the porch.

The two ideas could be expressed as two separate sentences, but they are more effectively expressed in a complex sentence. In a complex sentence the two ideas can be combined in a way that shows their cause-and-effect relationship. Notice how the word *because* explains to the reader the cause of Roger's problems. What follows the cause is the effect: Roger spent a week sleeping on the porch.

In the sentence about Roger, the word *because* is called a **subordinating conjunction**. That might sound like a puzzling term, but it is simply a type of word that will help you show the relationships between your ideas. Adverb clauses always begin with subordinating conjunctions.

Subordinating Conjunctions

Time	Cause and Effect	Contrast
• after • before • as soon as • as • when • until • while	• because • since • if • even though	• although • while • though • whereas • unless

Here is another example of two simple sentences that might be combined into a single complex sentence with an adverb clause:

Simple Sentence	Combined Sentence
The jury didn't believe the woman. The woman said that she killed her husband to prevent aliens from torturing him.	The jury didn't believe the woman when she said that she killed her husband to prevent aliens from torturing him.

As a writer, you have a choice to open a sentence with an adverb clause or end your sentence with an adverb clause. Notice that when the adverb clause comes at the beginning, you use a comma to separate it from the rest of the sentence; but when the adverb clause comes at the end of the sentence, no comma is necessary.

Complex Sentences Made Easy *(cont.)*

Directions: Circle the subordinating conjunctions and underline any adverb clauses.

1. Although he was tired, mad, and hungry, the sophomore, a hard working young man, quietly read his textbook, a 5-inch thick tome on American history.

2. Randy loves to read; however, he cannot stand Hemingway.

3. Mr. Johnson's teenage son has a brand new car even though he does not have a job.

4. When he found out that the price of the buffet did not include a soft drink, Stan settled for a cup of gravy.

5. When Luke made homemade ice cream, he didn't realize that he had mistakenly added black olives instead of blueberries.

6. Since there are 85 billion different possibilities for the first four moves of a chess game, alternative moves are not hard to find.

7. If you add kiwifruit to gelatin, it will not gel.

8. When he began using his phone book to call random numbers, Joe's friends knew that he was desperate for a date to the dance.

Sentence Combining: Combine the following sentences into a single complex sentence with at least one adverb clause.

1. Pedro spent all night on it. He was unable to finish his project, a solar-powered toothbrush.

   _____

   _____

2. Ron wants to find a cure for the common cold and for hiccups. He then wants to retire and live in Florida.

   _____

   _____

3. The teacher announced that the test was cancelled. The class cheered.

   _____

   _____

Practice 1: Look over the list of 40 topics on pages 65–67. On a separate piece of paper, write at least eight complex sentences with adverb clauses on one or multiple topics

Practice 2: At random, select a noun and a verb from the lists on page 63, and combine the words by using them in a complex sentence with an adverb clause. You may alter the noun or verb; however, you must use the noun as a noun and the verb as a verb. On a separate piece of paper, write eight simple sentences with eight different random combinations of nouns and verbs.

Bonus: Find an example of a sentence that uses an adverb clause, either in a work of fiction you are reading or in a newspaper or magazine article/ad. On a separate piece of paper, write down the sentence and the author and title of the source from which you got it. Underline the adverb clauses.

Write Your Own Complex Sentences with Adverb Clauses

A complex sentence is really not all that mind-boggling. In fact, the real purpose of complex sentences is to combine more than one idea into a single clear, logical sentence.

Every adverb clause begins with a subordinating conjunction. As you can see in the box below, subordinating conjunctions look like everyday, run-of-the-mill words. In reality, however, they are very important words that work like railroad signals to help the reader follow your train of thought. For example, notice the difference in the following two incomplete statements:

➡ Because Max likes to play Ping-Pong . . .

➡ Although Max likes to play Ping-Pong . . .

Except for the first word, the two statements are exactly the same—but the one word changes the entire direction and meaning of the rest of the sentences. Even without knowing the ending of the first sentence, you know that it must have something to do with an effect of Max loving Ping-Pong, such as "Because Max likes to play Ping-Pong, he never leaves home without his paddle." The subordinating conjunction *because* is a signal word that lets the reader know that an effect is coming. In the second sentence, you can predict that the second part of the sentence will have something to do with a contrast to Max liking Ping-Pong, such as "Although Max likes to play Ping-Pong, he would rather play lawn darts." The reason you can predict this is because *although* is a subordinating conjunction that signals a contrast in ideas. (See the *Subordinating Conjunctions* chart on page 42.)

Now, look at the step-by-step instructions box below.

Step by Step: How to Write a Sentence with an Adverb Clause

Step 1: Write a complete sentence:

Joe ate twelve bananas.

Step 2: Add a subordinating conjunction to the beginning of the sentence to make it a clause:

After Joe ate twelve bananas

Step 3: Transform the adverb clause into a complex sentence by adding an independent clause that completes the thought:

After Joe ate twelve bananas, he had a sudden impulse to climb the elm tree in his front yard.

Excuse Generator: 256 Quick Excuses

In the table of excuses below, four separate sentences are broken up into four parts that explain why I didn't do my homework. If you select a row at random from A, B, C, and D, the words can be combined to form a complex sentence with an adverb clause. There are a total of 256 possible combinations of sentences. For example, if you selected row 3 for column A, row 1 for column B, row 3 for column C, and row 4 for column D, the sentence you would have would be:

➡ I didn't do my homework because this morning my wicked step-sister chewed up my last roll of toilet paper.

Directions: Select your own rows at random from A, B, C, and D, and write two complex sentences with subordinating conjunctions below:

1. Row _____ Column A   Row _____ Column B   Row _____ Column C   Row _____ Column D

   I didn't do my homework because _____

   _____

2. Row _____ Column A   Row _____ Column B   Row _____ Column C   Row _____ Column D

   I didn't do my homework because _____

   _____

I didn't do my homework because . . .			
A. When?	**B. Who?**	**C. Did What?**	**D. To What?**
Just before the bell rang,	my wicked step-sister	vomited on	my new state-of-the-art computer.
Late last night,	my pet chihuahua	snatched	my award-winning origami creations.
This morning,	an extraterrestrial	chewed up	my one-of-a-kind Elvis jumpsuit.
Four minutes ago,	my meddling guardian	demolished	my last roll of toilet paper.

Add your own words for A, B, C, and D in the above boxes. If you fill in all 16 boxes and make combinations using all 32 boxes, there are 4,096 possible sentence combinations. Write three below.

1. _____

2. _____

3. _____

Complex Sentences with an Adjective Clause: Everything Is Relative

A complex sentence is a sentence in which at least two ideas are combined into a single sentence. So, even though it's called a "complex" sentence, it's really a pretty simple concept. For example, look at the following sentence:

➡ Susan, who loves to swim in freezing water, recently joined the Polar Bear Club.

The two ideas expressed in the sentence are:

1. Susan recently joined the Polar Bear Club.
2. Susan loves to swim in freezing water.

The two ideas could be expressed as two separate sentences, but the two ideas are more clearly and concisely expressed in a complex sentence.

In the sentence about Susan, the word *who* is called a **relative pronoun**. That might sound like an odd term, but it is simply a type of word that will help you combine ideas to write clear and concise sentences. Adjective clauses always begin with relative pronouns.

◇◇◇Relative Pronouns◇◇◇

• who	• whom	• whose	• which	• that	• when	• where

In the following examples, notice that before each adjective clause is a noun or pronoun. The adjective clause tells more about that noun or pronoun.

➡ Bill, who loves to bowl, is lobbying to have a bowling alley installed in his high school's basement.

➡ The family that lives down the street just bought a 300-pound pet gorilla.

➡ The man always walked down the middle of the street carrying a multicolored umbrella, which shielded him from the rain.

Adjective clauses are either *essential* or *non-essential*. An essential clause is one that must be included to make the meaning of the sentence complete. Essential clauses require no commas. A non-essential clause is one that gives extra information. Non-essential clauses are offset by commas.

Essential Clause
➡ The man who is wearing the bad toupee is the judge.

Nonessential Clause
➡ The judge, who is an unemployed circus clown, gave us a good score on our science project.

Complex Sentences with an Adjective Clause: Everything Is Relative *(cont.)*

Directions: Underline any adjective clauses in the following sentences:

1. Nora, who is a big Alfred Hitchcock fan, has seen *Psycho* 112 times.

2. Jesse James, who had spent too many nights sleeping next to his horse, was overdue for a bath.

3. The new can opener, which we bought as a present for our parents' anniversary, no longer works.

4. Dracula made a withdrawal from the blood bank and went to the park to eat his lunch.

5. Jenny, who loves to bowl, and Andy, who loves to eat chili, are now spending a lot of time together.

6. The suspect in the string of vending machine robberies, who was not very smart, paid his $400 bail entirely in quarters.

7. The stegosaurus, which was 30 feet long, had a brain the size of a walnut.

8. Pompeii, which was hidden for 17 centuries, was buried when Mount Vesuvius erupted in 79 A.D.

Sentence Combining: Combine the following sentences into a single complex sentence with at least one adjective clause.

1. In 1940 a tornado showered gold coins over a Russian town. The tornado uncovered buried gold.

   _____

   _____

2. Joe enjoys novels. He enjoys novels that feature fearless, adventurous characters.

   _____

   _____

3. The mayor proposed an ordinance against polka dancing. The mayor did not want to get re-elected.

   _____

   _____

Practice 1: Look over the list of 40 topics on pages 65–67. On a separate piece of paper, write at least eight complex sentences with adjective clauses on one or multiple topics.

Practice 2: At random, select a noun and a verb from the lists on page 63, and combine the words by using them in a complex sentence with an adjective clause. You may alter the noun or verb; however, you must use the noun as a noun and the verb as a verb. On a separate piece of paper, write eight simple sentences with eight different random combinations of nouns and verbs.

Bonus: Find an example of a sentence that uses an adjective clause, either in a work of fiction you are reading or in a newspaper or magazine article/ad. On a separate piece of paper, write down the sentence and the author and title of the source from which you got it. Underline the adjective clauses.

Write Your Own Complex Sentences with Adjective Clauses

It is not hard to include complex sentences with adjective clauses in your own writing.

Step by Step: How to Write a Sentence with an Adjective Clause

Step 1: Write a simple sentence:

Isaac wrote his essay on a word processor.

Step 2: Look at the nouns in the sentence, and generate ideas for how to give more information about them. Begin each of your ideas with a relative pronoun.

Relative Pronouns: who, whom, whose, which, that, when, where

Isaac, who is known for his poor spelling

essay that had 450 spelling errors

word processor that did not have a spell-checker

Step 3: Revise and expand your sentence by adding the adjective clauses.

Isaac, who is known for his poor spelling, wrote an essay that had 450 spelling errors on a word processor that did not have a spell-checker.

Writing Activity

Television Series Proposal

Follow the instructions in the step-by-step box to write your own complex sentences with adjective clauses. Write at least three proposals for new television dramas and/or comedies. Include information about the key characters and the setting of your shows.

Here is an example of a proposal for a television situation comedy:

Jason Jibson, who is an avid collector of tarantulas, manages a hair salon in New York where the female workers are constantly being frightened by huge, hairy spiders that have escaped from Jason's cages.

1. _____

_____

2. _____

_____

3. _____

_____

Compound Sentences: No "*Ifs,*" but Plenty of "*Ands,*" "*Buts,*" and "*Ors*"

A compound sentence is a handy way to combine two related ideas into a single sentence.

➡ Our neighborhood ice-cream man loves Elvis, and his ice-cream truck plays "Hound Dog."

The two related ideas in the above sentence are:

1. Our neighborhood ice-cream man loves Elvis.
2. His ice-cream truck plays "Hound Dog."

The two ideas could be expressed as two separate ideas, but the two ideas are more effectively expressed in a compound sentence, because in a compound sentence the two ideas can be "compounded" or combined in a way that shows their relationship.

In the above sentence about the ice-cream man, the word that combines the two ideas is *and*. *And* is a **coordinating conjunction**. Compound sentences usually contain coordinating conjunctions. Coordinating conjunctions are easy to remember because they are either two- or three-letter words: *for, and, nor, but, or, yet, so*. These magnificent seven words can be easily remembered using the acronym "fanboys":

For, **A**nd, **N**or, **B**ut, **O**r, **Y**et, **S**o

Coordinating conjunctions work like traffic signs to help the reader follow your thinking. Below is a listing of coordinating conjunctions, grouped according to the type of signal they give the reader:

Coordinating Conjunctions

Cause and Effect	Addition	Contrast
• for • so	• and	• but • yet • or • nor

Notice how the two sentences below begin the same way but finish differently because of the signal given by the coordinating conjunction:

➡ Bill is taking October 4th off from work, for it's the anniversary of the television premiere of *Leave It To Beaver*.

➡ Bill is taking October 4th off from work, but he is coming in early to work the following morning.

Comma Note: Use a comma before a coordinating conjunction when writing a compound sentence.

Compound Sentences: No "*Ifs*," but Plenty of "*Ands*," "*Buts*," and "*Ors*" *(cont.)*

Directions: For the following sentences, place a **Y** next to the compound sentences and an **N** next to the sentences that are not compound. Circle all coordinating conjunctions.

_____ 1. Only seven out of 100 people admit to ever flossing their teeth with their hair, but one in four admits to having picked his or her teeth with a match.

_____ 2. Men are more likely than women to squeeze their pimples.

_____ 3. Hershey's supplies M&Ms to the White House free of charge, but they supply only peanut-flavored ones.

_____ 4. Rhode Island is a small state geographically, but its population is twice that of Alaska.

_____ 5. The hack sack was invented in Turkey, but it is most popular in the Unites States.

_____ 6. Tracy and Tom have worked for five months to housebreak their pet armadillo.

_____ 7. Bill's English teacher loves word games, so today he asked his students to name the only U.S. state with a one syllable name.

_____ 8. A housefly regurgitates its food, and then it eats it again.

Sentence Combining: Combine the following sentences into a single compound sentence.

1. Sheila spent three hours writing her essay. She didn't spend any time proofreading her essay.

    _____

    _____

2. Our computer is not working. Don't send us any e-mail.

    _____

    _____

3. In the morning Ron always sings Irish ballads. In the evening he always sings patriotic hymns.

    _____

    _____

Practice 1: Look over the list of 40 topics on pages 65–67. On a separate piece of paper, write at least eight compound sentences on one or multiple topics

Practice 2: At random, select a noun and a verb from the lists on page 63, and combine the words by using them in a compound sentence. You may alter the noun or verb; however, you must use the noun as a noun and the verb as a verb. On a separate piece of paper, write eight sentences with eight different random combinations of nouns and verbs.

Bonus: Find an example of a compound sentence with a coordinating conjunction, either in a work of fiction you are reading or in a newspaper or magazine article/ad. On a separate piece of paper, write down the sentence and the author and title of the source from which you got it.

Write Your Own Compound Sentences

What do the following sentences have in common?

➡ Women spend an average of 164 minutes per day reading; men spend an average of 150 minutes per day reading.

➡ More that 16 billion hot dogs per year are sold in the United States, and July is National Hot Dog Month.

➡ The United States leads the world in hot-dog sales, but it is not even in the top 10 in mustard sales.

They are all compound sentences. Using compound sentences is an easy way to combine two related ideas into a single sentence.

Step by Step: How to Write a Compound Sentence

Step 1: Write a simple sentence:

> Our neighborhood ice-cream man is a big Elvis fan.

Step 2: Elaborate on the simple sentence by adding another complete idea. Connect your idea to the first simple sentence using a coordinating conjunction that shows either cause and effect, addition, or contrast. (See the *Coordinating Conjunctions* chart on page 49.)

> Our neighborhood ice-cream man is a big Elvis fan, and his ice-cream truck plays "Hound Dog."

> Our neighborhood ice-cream man is a big Elvis fan, but his ice-cream truck plays a medley of Beatles tunes.

Writing Activity

Holiday Cards

Follow the instructions in the step-by-step box to write your own compound sentences. Think of currently existing holidays, or create new holidays. Write three separate compound sentences for three separate greeting cards that celebrate your holidays. Any anniversary, birthday, or other historical date can be used as a holiday.

Here is an example:

> Today is Elvis' birthday, so don't be cruel.

Holiday 1: _____

_____

Holiday 2: _____

_____

Holiday 3: _____

_____

Compound-Complex Sentences: Putting It All Together

A compound-complex sentence is a sentence in which at least three ideas are combined into a single sentence. For example, look at the following sentence:

➡ After Blake buys a set of bagpipes, he plans to join a band, and he hopes to be famous someday.

The three ideas expressed in the sentence are:

1. Blake plans to buy a set of bagpipes.

2. Blake plans to join a band.

3. Blake hopes to be famous someday.

These three ideas could be expressed in three separate sentences, but the relationship between the ideas is best expressed when the sentences are combined into a single, logical sentence.

Every compound-complex sentence features at least two different kinds of connecting words that work to show the relationships between the ideas. For example, in the following sentence the words *who* and *then* connect the ideas.

➡ Stan, who is too cheap to buy lip balm, rubs his finger over the exterior of his nose to absorb his skin's oils; then, he rubs his finger on his lips, giving them a dose of his own natural moisturizer.

The boxes below show the two different sets of connecting words. Compound-complex sentences use at least one word from each set.

Set 1

Subordinating Conjunctions: after, before, as soon as, when, until, while, because, since, if, even though, although, while, though, whereas, unless

Relative Pronouns: who, whom, whose, which, that, when, or where

---

Set 2

Coordinating Conjunctions: for, and, nor, but, or, yet, so

Conjunctive Adverbs: also, as a result, consequently, for example, furthermore, however, moreover, otherwise, still, then, therefore, thus

---

Punctuation Note: When using a coordinating conjunction to connect two complete thoughts, use a comma before the coordinating conjunction.

➡ The United States leads the world in hot-dog sales, but it is not even in the top 10 in mustard sales.

When using a conjunctive adverb to connect two complete thoughts, use a semicolon before the conjunctive adverb and a comma after it.

➡ The United States leads the world in hot dog sales; however, it is not even in the top 10 in mustard sales.

Compound-Complex Sentences: Putting It All Together *(cont.)*

Directions: First, circle all of the Set 1 Connecting Words (from page 52) and draw a box around the Set 2 Connecting Words (from page 52). Then, determine which sentences below are compound-complex sentences by underlining the connecting words.

1. Dr. Seuss wrote *Green Eggs and Ham*, which is his all-time best seller, when his publisher challenged him to write a book using only 50 different words.

2. Shelly told Garry that she could not go out with him on Friday night because her hair dryer is broken, and she needs more time to organize her stamp collection.

3. John's mother had been patient with his at-home experimentation; however, she put her foot down when he decided to see if it was true that cat urine glows under a black light.

4. When the Pentagon in Arlington, Virginia, was constructed in the 1940s, the State of Virginia still had segregation laws on the books that required separate toilet facilities for blacks and whites; therefore, today it has twice as many bathrooms as necessary.

5. The trouble began when Bill told a small lie about his ability jump from high places; as a result, he now has a broken left leg and right arm.

Sentence Combining: Combine the following sentences into a single simple sentence.

1. His car runs. The air conditioning is broken. The 8-track tape player plays only in reverse.

_____

_____

2. The substitute teacher forgot to assign the homework. The substitute teacher was having a rough day. The class had twice as much homework the following night.

_____

_____

3. Your computer continues to break down. You should have the hard drive repaired. You should buy a new computer.

_____

_____

Practice 1: Look over the list of 40 topics on pages 65–67. On a separate piece of paper, write at least eight compound-complex sentences on one or multiple topics.

Practice 2: At random, select a noun and a verb from the lists on page 63. Combine the words by using them in a compound-complex sentence. You may alter the noun or verb; however, you must use the noun as a noun and the verb as a verb. On a separate piece of paper, write eight compound-complex sentences with eight different random combinations of nouns and verbs.

Bonus: Find an example of a compound-complex sentence, either in a work of fiction you are reading or in a newspaper or magazine article/ad. On a separate piece of paper, write down the sentence and the author and title of the source from which you got it.

Write Your Own
Compound-Complex Sentences

What do the following sentences have in common?

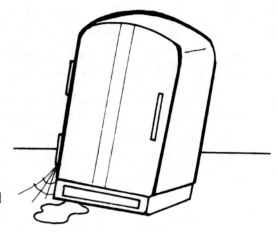

➡ Larry was late for first period again because his waffle iron malfunctioned, and it caused a three-alarm fire on Maple Street.

➡ Joe does not like to clean his refrigerator, but he hates to scrape mold off his pudding before he eats it; therefore, he is planning to clean out his refrigerator at least once a week.

➡ His hands in his pockets, the sales representative, who worked on commission, talked with the customers, and he hoped to convince them to buy his product, a solar cigarette lighter.

They are compound-complex sentences, a type of sentence that combines at least three separate ideas into a single, logical sentence.

It is not hard to include compound-complex sentences in your own writing. Look at the step-by-step instructions box below.

Step by Step: How to Write a Compound-Complex Sentence

Step 1: Begin by writing three related sentences about a common subject:

Tycho Brahe was a 16th century astronomer.

Tycho Brahe lost his nose in a duel with one of his students over a mathematical computation.

Tycho Brahe wore a silver nose for the rest of his life.

Step 2: Combine the three ideas by selecting at least one connecting word from Set 1 and one connecting word from Set 2. (See page 52.)

Step 3: Combine the ideas into a single clear sentence:

Tycho Brahe, who was a 16th century astronomer, lost his nose in a duel with one of his students over a mathematical computation; as a result, he wore a silver nose for the rest of his life.

Write Your Own
Compound-Complex Sentences *(cont.)*

Writing Activity

Game Show or Reality Show Pitch

Write a proposal for a new game show or reality show. Be creative, but make sure that you write your proposal in the form of a compound-complex sentence.

Here are a few examples:

The contestants, who are wearing animal costumes, must make the most authentic animal noises; however, they are not told until the show begins which animal they will be impersonating.

Left on desert island, where there is nothing but rocks and sand, the contestants, a son-in-law and his mother-in-law, must survive for three days on a single glass of water and a pound of trail mix; furthermore, the contestants are chained together at the ankles.

_____

_____

_____

_____

_____

_____

_____

_____

_____

_____

_____

_____

_____

Two Feet on the Cold, Hard Ground: Using Concrete, Specific Word Choice and Sensory Words

Your reader is able to think about abstract ideas like love, freedom, and justice—but your reader also has two feet that stand on the cold, hard ground; therefore, he or she is attracted by specific, concrete details. If you want to write about love, that's fine, but make sure that you include concrete words and examples to go with the abstract. Talk about the sweat dripping down your back as you attempt to ask someone for a date, or talk about running your hand through the hair of the one you love. Also, make your words specific. Don't talk about "a tree," talk about "a towering sequoia"; don't talk about "a car," talk about a "red 1964 Corvette."

In addition to concrete words and details, use sensory words to create a picture in the mind of your reader. Sensory words should describe more than just what things look like. They should also describe the sounds, smells, tastes, or feelings of things. Sensory words will help you write sentences that do more than just "tell" the reader; sensory words help you "show" the reader.

Cafeteria Craziness

Read the two paragraphs below. Both paragraphs have the same topic sentence: *We don't have enough time to eat lunch.* Which one do you think makes the best use of concrete, specific word choice and sensory words to make its point?

Paragraph #1

We don't have enough time to eat lunch. Thirty minutes is not enough time to make it through the long lines, let alone consume your food. Instead of savoring our food and our friends' conversation, we must eat our food like animals. Tardy after tardy stack up as we attempt to finish our meals and make it back to class on time. Rush, rush, rush is all we do. It is virtually impossible to eat in the short amount of time we have for lunch.

Paragraph #2

We don't have enough time to eat lunch. Imagine a speedway with cars frantically pitting for a little go-go juice and some fresh traction. Now imagine a school cafeteria with students racing towards the lunch lines for some awful slop that rats won't touch, just to get a little nourishment before the bell tolls, reverberating down the narrow corridors with a frightening sternness. A pig's trough could be the only equivalent to the tables where the starving adolescents sit and engulf their food in hearty bites without a breath taken or word spoken. A low, rumbling murmur is present but is overpowered by the scraping of plastic forks against trays and slopping of the "mystery meat." Conversations consist only of a nod of the head, a grunt from within, or a wink of the eye.

Two Feet on the Cold, Hard Ground: Using Concrete, Specific Word Choice and Sensory Words *(cont.)*

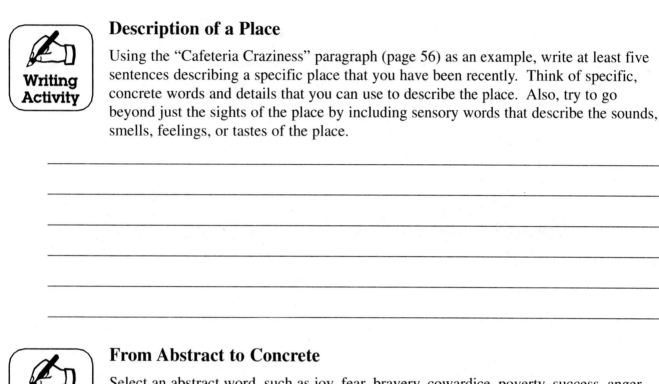

Description of a Place

Using the "Cafeteria Craziness" paragraph (page 56) as an example, write at least five sentences describing a specific place that you have been recently. Think of specific, concrete words and details that you can use to describe the place. Also, try to go beyond just the sights of the place by including sensory words that describe the sounds, smells, feelings, or tastes of the place.

_____

_____

_____

_____

_____

_____

From Abstract to Concrete

Select an abstract word, such as joy, fear, bravery, cowardice, poverty, success, anger, frustration, or love. Then, write a sentence in which you make the abstract word come to life by describing a specific, concrete scene that relates to the meaning of the abstract term. Do not, however, mention the abstract word in your sentence. Include concrete, specific word choice and sensory words in the description of your scene.

Here is an example:

Abstract Word: _____ Fear _____

After throwing the enormous, dripping spit-wad, the student cowered under his desk as the pounding of the angry teacher's approaching footsteps reverberated through the classroom.

Abstract Word: _____

_____

_____

_____

_____

You Came, You Saw, and You Conquered Parallelism

When Abraham Lincoln concluded his Gettysburg Address, he used parallelism to make sure he ended on a strong note, saying:

> *"...this government of the people, by the people, for the people, shall not perish from this Earth."*

Parallelism is more than simply the repetition of words; it's the repetition of word patterns. In Lincoln's conclusion you hear the repetition of the word *people*, but you should also hear the repetition of the prepositional phrases beginning with *of*, *by*, and *for*.

Parallelism is a big word for a simple concept. Our brains naturally work to recognize patterns. That is one reason that parallelism is an effective technique for writing sentences. Look at the following groups of words and see if you can tell which of the groups follows the same pattern.

Group A	Group B	Group C	Group D
Eating	before breakfast	who loves reading	It's a spoon
To drink	during lunch	who likes writing	It's a fork
Sleeping	after dinner	who tolerates public speaking	It's a spork

All the groups are parallel except for Group A. In order to make Group A parallel, we would simply need to change *drink* to its *-ing* form *drinking* so that it fits the pattern.

After correcting Group A to make it parallel, we could write sentences from each of the groups that feature parallel structure:

Group A: Eating, drinking, and sleeping are all that John seems to care about.

Group B: Joe enjoys flossing before breakfast, during lunch, and after dinner.

Group C: Mary is a professional wrestler who loves reading, who likes writing, and who tolerates public speaking.

Group D: This new utensil is amazing: it's a spoon, it's a fork—it's a spork.

Parallelism makes a person's writing more economical, more logical, more elaborate, and more pleasing to the ear. It also makes things easy to remember and easy to follow because of its rhythm and logical structure.

You Came, You Saw, and You Conquered Parallelism *(cont.)*

Writing Activity

Autobiographical Sentences

Read the following sentences and try to imitate the patterns of each by including new details that apply to your life, your interests, and your experiences.

Sentence 1: Three things that you did in the past.

I climbed Mount Everest, ran a marathon, and built a log home before I slipped in the shower and broke my leg.

_____

_____

Sentence 2: Three things you did leading up to something. (Use *–ing* words.)

Removing a large glob of gum from my mouth, rolling it up in a ball, and stopping to think a moment, I couldn't decide whether to deposit it behind my ear or under my desk.

_____

_____

Sentence 3: Three things about the kind of person you are right now. (Use *who* to introduce each.)

I am the kind of student who loves to listen to music, who loves to shop for music, but who hates to sing.

_____

_____

Sentence 4: Three things that you like to do. (Use *–ing* words followed by *that*.)

I love to write, styling sonorous sentences that startle the stubborn, crafting crackling clauses that confound the cautious, and forging fantastic phrases that frighten the fainthearted.

_____

_____

Counterfeit Sentences Game

In the Counterfeit Sentences Game, students try their hand at creating sentences that sound like those written by professional writers.

Materials

- a group of 4–6 players
- a copy of a novel
- several blank sheets of paper or 3" x 5" cards
- a pen or pencil for each player

Object of the Game

Score points by writing sentences that sound so professionally written that they could be in a published novel.

Game Rules and Instructions

1. Select a judge for the first round. The judge rotates each round, so everyone will have a chance to be the judge.

2. The judge, without showing the players, selects a sentence of at least 10 words from a novel. It's usually best to select a sentence that is not in quotations marks, since dialogue sentences often don't make much sense out of context. The judge writes the sentence on a slip of paper and underlines a noun and a verb from the sentence.

3. Next, the judge tells the players the title and author of the novel; the judge also writes the noun and the verb from the sentence on the white/blackboard.

4. Without showing each other, each player then writes a sentence of at least 10 words on a slip of paper that sounds like it might be a plausible sentence based on the title/author of the novel. The goal of each player is to make the other players think that his or her sentence is the actual sentence. Each player gives his/her sentence to the judge, sentence side down, when finished.

5. The judge then mixes up the slips of paper, which include the slip of paper with the actual sentence. The judge then reads all the sentences aloud in no particular order.

6. The judge asks each player to state the sentence that he or she thinks is the actual sentence and records each player's guess. Next, the judge announces the actual sentence. Writers earn a point each time another player selects their sentence as the real one; players also earn a point for guessing the actual sentence.

7. After recording the scoring for the round, the position of judge rotates to another player who has not yet been a judge. The judge for the last round now becomes a player for the next round.

8. Play as many rounds as there are players in the group. The player with the most points after the last player has had a chance to be the judge is declared the winner.

Note: See page 62 for an example of the Counterfeit Sentences Game.

Random Combo Game

In the Random Combo Game, players write creative sentences using a given noun and verb. To win, they must write a sentence that stands out as more zany, more crazy, or more off-beat than the competition.

Materials

- a group of 4–8 people
- several slips of paper or 3" x 5" cards
- a pen or pencil for each player
- the list of 35 nouns and 35 verbs (page 63)

Object of the Game

The object is to score points by writing the most wacky, off-beat, zany, and correct sentences.

Game Rules and Instructions

1. Select a judge for the first round. The judge rotates each round, so everyone will have a chance to be the judge.

2. At random the judge selects a noun and a verb from the list of 35 nouns and verbs and writes the noun and verb on the white/blackboard.

3. Without showing anyone, each player then writes a single sentence of at least 10 words that includes the noun and the verb. The players may alter the noun and verb, but they must use the noun as a noun and the verb as a verb. The goal of each player is to make the judge select his/her sentences as the best, most creative sentence. (To qualify as a winning sentence, a sentence must also be a complete sentence.) Each player gives his/her sentence to the judge, sentence side down, when finished.

4. Without looking at any of the sentences, the judge then mixes up the slips of paper.

5. The judge then reads each sentence aloud in no particular order without any comments being made by the players.

6. Once the judge has read all the sentences, he/she then explains his/her selection for the winning sentence, telling the players why the one sentence stood out. The judge then records a point for the winning sentence writer.

7. After recording the scoring for the round, the position of judge rotates to another player who has not yet been a judge. The judge for the last round now becomes a player for the next round.

8. Play as many rounds as there are players in the group. The player with the most points after the last player has had a chance to be the judge is declared the winner.

> **Note:** See page 62 for an example of the Random Combo Game.

Sentence Games in Action

Counterfeit Sentences Game

Here is an example of five sentences from a game of Counterfeit Sentences. The noun given by the judge was *people* and the verb was *to smell*. Four of the sentences were written by players, and one was written by John Steinbeck in his novel *The Grapes of Wrath*. Can you tell which is the real sentence? Circle the number of your choice.

1. The people could not avoid smelling the decaying carcass of the dead turtle that they found in the road.

2. The people came out of their houses and smelled the hot stinging air and covered their noses from it.

3. At night the people smelled the aroma of the freshly cut wheat that filled the air.

4. As the breakfast cooked, the people smelled the wonderful aroma of frying sausage, eggs, potatoes, and buttermilk pancakes.

5. Never before had the people smelled anything like the pungent aroma of the burning garbage.

❖❖❖❖❖

Random Combo Game

Here is an example of five sentences from a game of Random Combo. The noun given by the judge was "vegetarian lasagna" and the verb was "to tackle." Pretend you are the judge. Which sentence would you choose as the winner, and why? Circle the number of your choice.

1. Ron tackled his little brother when he laughed at Ron who had dressed up as a vegetarian lasagna for Halloween.

2. The Italian chef tackled the thief who tried to steal his famous vegetarian lasagna recipe.

3. The 85-year-old grandmother tackled the German shepherd as he tried to leap up onto the kitchen counter to grab her fresh-baked vegetarian lasagna.

4. His mouth stuffed with vegetarian lasagna, French bread, and green beans, the football player threatened to tackle anyone who dared to even look at his dessert.

5. Joe's mother tackled him and rubbed his face in a pan of vegetarian lasagna when he came home late for dinner last night.

Nouns and Verbs Lists

— Nouns *(with modifiers)* —

1. baby gorilla
2. bowling trophy
3. hairy big toe
4. pack of bubble gum
5. refrigerator magnet
6. broken clock radio
7. crazed English teacher
8. substitute teacher
9. low-fat strawberry yogurt
10. automatic garage door
11. toasted tuna sandwich
12. vegetarian lasagna
13. frozen TV dinner
14. annoying phone solicitor
15. public water fountain
16. ping-pong paddle
17. Halloween costume
18. petting zoo
19. electric guitar
20. psychedelic yo-yo
21. blood-thirsty vampire
22. three-story doghouse
23. enemy soldier
24. expensive plastic surgeon
25. plastic paper clip
26. cotton candy
27. angry librarian
28. radio talk-show host
29. gap-toothed flyweight champion
30. computer game
31. excited game-show contestant
32. heavy-metal rock star
33. toupee-wearing used car salesman
34. red suspenders
35. stuntman

— Verbs —

1. yodel
2. throw
3. climb
4. destroy
5. erupt
6. fly
7. investigate
8. jump
9. kick
10. tape
11. march
12. nag
13. ransack
14. scream
15. burp
16. guzzle
17. chew
18. tackle
19. untangle
20. race
21. whistle
22. argue
23. swim
24. panic
25. forget
26. discuss
27. hurtle
28. debate
29. choke
30. laugh
31. drive
32. shop
33. sprint
34. read
35. slice

Forty Terrific Topics Game

In the Forty Terrific Topics Game, players must write a sentence based on a given topic. The goal of each player is to write a sentence that stands out from the crowd.

Materials

- a group of 4–8 people
- several slips of paper or 3" x 5" cards
- a pen or pencil for each player
- the list of Forty Terrific Topics (pages 65–67)

Object of the Game

The object is to score points by writing the most wacky, off-beat, zany, and correct sentences based on one of the Forty Terrific Topics.

Game Rules and Instructions

1. Select a judge for the first round. The judge rotates each round, so everyone will have a chance to be the judge.

2. The judge selects a topic from the list of 40 Terrific Topics and reads the topic aloud to the group.

3. Without showing anyone, each player then writes a single sentence of at least 10 words on the stated topic. The goal of each player is to make the judge select his/her sentence as the best, most creative sentence. (To qualify as a winning sentence, a sentence must also be a complete sentence, and it must be on the assigned topic.) Each player gives his/her sentence to the judge, sentence side down, when finished.

4. Without looking at any of the sentences, the judge then mixes up the slips of paper.

5. The judge then reads each sentence aloud in no particular order without any comments being made by the players.

6. Once the judge has read all the sentences, he/she then explains his/her selection for the winning sentence, telling the players why the one sentence stood out. The judge then records a point for the winning sentence writer.

7. After recording the scoring for the round, the position of judge rotates to another player who has not yet been a judge. The judge for the last round now becomes a player for the next round.

8. Play as many rounds as there are players in the group. The player with the most points after the last player has had a chance to be the judge is declared the winner.

Forty Terrific Topics Game *(cont.)*

Topics

1. Write down the name of your favorite sitcom, and create a new plot for an episode. Write a sentence summary of the key events in your episode. Don't forget to mention the characters, the setting, and the conflict that will drive your episode.

2. Write down the name of a holiday, and write a sentence for a greeting card that celebrates that holiday. Any anniversary, birthday, or other historical date can be used as a holiday.

3. Write down the name of a new holiday of your own creation, and write a sentence for an ad promoting the new holiday. Any historical date or birthday can become a holiday.

4. Write down the name of a product, and write a sentence in which you allude to a historical event or person while advertising the product.

5. Your 400-page autobiography has just been published. Write a sentence from page 100 of your autobiography.

6. Write down the name of a physical object you value, and write a sentence in which you describe the object.

7. Write a news lead for a tabloid story. These stories frequently deal with strange animal or human oddities, aliens, fads, life-after-death, or crime.

8. Write a sentence explaining your idea for a new game show or reality show.

9. Write a lead for a news story that might appear 10 years from now. Tell the who, what, when, and where of your story.

10. Write a new ad slogan for an existing product. Consider using alliteration, rhyme, or a pun.

11. Write a country song lyric. Think pick-up trucks, dogs, and cowboy hats.

12. Write a pop song lyric. Think young love, sunny days, and fast cars.

13. Write a pangram (a sentence containing every letter in the alphabet at least once).

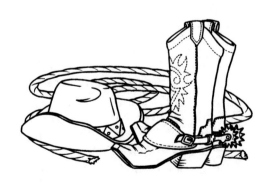

The quick, brown fox jumps over the lazy dog.

Forty Terrific Topics Game *(cont.)*

Topics *(cont.)*

14. Write a single-syllable sentence haiku. Each word should be a single syllable. Write the sentence in three lines of verse: the first 5 syllables, the second 7, and the third 5. The lines don't have to rhyme, but they should capture some kind of image.

15. Write a sentence haiku. Write the sentence in three lines of verse: the first 5 syllables, the second 7, and the third 5. The lines don't have to rhyme, but they should capture some kind of image.

16. Write the opening sentence of a horror novel. Think cemeteries, dark rainy nights, and ghosts.

17. Write the opening sentence of a romance novel. Think exotic locations, roses, and love-at-first-sight.

18. Write the opening sentence of a sci-fi novel. Think robots, technology gone bad, and space travel.

19. Write the opening sentence of a western novel. Think dusty trails, horses, six guns, saloons, and gold strikes.

20. Write the opening sentence of a crime/detective/mystery novel. Think hard time, bank robbery, and fingerprints.

21. Write the opening sentence of a short story about a character in conflict with himself/herself. Think about difficult decision or complex problem the character must solve.

22. Write the opening sentence of a short story about a character in conflict with nature. Think mountains, forest, sea, weather, and natural disasters.

23. Write the opening sentence of a short story about a protagonist in conflict with an antagonist. Think competitors, rivals, enemies, and good guys and bad guys.

24. Write a sentence in which you use hyperbole in talking about your life achievements. Exaggerate the truth to create outrageous claims or humorous situations.

25. Write a sentence in which you use understatement in talking about a historical event or person. Think about an event that changed the course of history and write as if it were no big deal.

26. Write down an abstract noun like *greed, love, poverty,* or *success*. Write a sentence in which you make this abstract idea concrete through description of a person, place, or event. Use specific language to show what this abstract idea looks like in real life.

27. Write the opening sentence of a children's story. Think animals, magic, and simple but precise words.

Forty Terrific Topics Game *(cont.)*

───────────────── **Topics** *(cont.)* ─────────────────

28. Write a description of a product as it might be described in a catalog. Make the inanimate object come alive by showing the reader how it can be used and how it will improve his/her life.

29. Write the text of your postcard from your dream vacation. Make them wish they were there by showing them what you are seeing, hearing, feeling, and doing.

30. Write a sentence using alliteration. The silent, slinking serpent slid across the cold concrete.

31. Write a sentence reviewing a restaurant in your hometown. Describe the sights, sounds, smells, and tastes of the place.

32. Write the first sentence of a letter complaining to a company about its product. Make sure to name the company and the product.

33. Write the first sentence of a first-person narrative in which a character is speaking in an angry tone about what has upset him or her. Use the pronoun *I*.

34. Write a rhyming couplet.

    After shooting 30 over par,
    Bill ran over his clubs with his car.

35. Write a sentence in which you describe your hometown from the perspective of the chamber of commerce. Think about the best qualities of your town and use words with positive connotation.

36. Write a sentence of at least 10 words without using the letter **e**. This type of sentence is called a lipogram.

    In most compositions this thing is hard to avoid, but in this composition you will not find it.

37. Write a sentence of at least 10 words in which every word is two syllables long, no more or no less.

    Gary enjoys every single Tuesday because after dinner, Mary prepares 20 tasty desserts.

38. Write a sentence of at least 10 words in which every word contains at least one letter **t**.

    After eating the burnt toast, Ted tossed the toaster, hitting the kitchen cabinet.

39. Write a sentence of at least 10 words in which every word is a single syllable.

    Gus is a big guy who likes to play chess.

40. Write a sentence speculating what might appear in your biography at your 10-year high-school reunion.

    Dream big.

Review of Sentence Skills

Pages 68–72 contain summaries and reviews of the 13 sentence structure skills (with word lists and examples).

Skill #1

Write a Simple Sentence
A simple sentence is made up of two parts: a subject (noun or pronoun) and a predicate (a verb).

Examples:

➡ Joe slept.

➡ After lunch, Jill went for a walk.

➡ Gregory went to the store and bought a new sofa.

Skill #2

Write a Simple Sentence with a Compound Subject and/or a Compound Predicate
When the subject of a sentence is made up of more than a single noun, it is called a compound subject.

Examples:

➡ John and Paul play the guitar while standing on their heads.

➡ After dinner, Jeff and Val spent the evening celebrating National Foot Care Month by cutting each other's toenails.

When the predicate of a sentence is made up of more than a single verb, it is called a compound predicate.

Examples:

➡ John plays the guitar and reads books while standing on his head.

➡ Fred sang a long song, wrote a long essay, and read a long poem yesterday.

Skill #3

Write a Sentence with Adjectives
Adjectives are words that describe nouns. Some examples are *green, eager, foggy, enormous, twelve,* and *energetic.*

Examples:

➡ The bossy, loud janitor ordered the student to stop eating in the hall.

➡ We only eat pancakes now that our old waffle iron is no longer working.

➡ Most colleges look for hardworking, self-motivated students.

Review of Sentence Skills *(cont.)*

Skill #4

Write a Sentence with an Adverb
Adverbs modify verbs by telling how the action is done. Adverbs frequently end in *ly*. Some examples are *eagerly, softly, aggressively,* and *enthusiastically.*

Examples:

➡ Calmly and quietly, Bill walked into the room.

➡ The football team fought tirelessly and tenaciously to win the game.

Skill #5

Write a Sentence with a Prepositional Phrase
Prepositional phrases always begin with a preposition and end with a noun or pronoun. Some examples of prepositions are *about, at, above, across, after, against, along, among, before, behind, below, beneath, beside, between, beyond, by, down, during, except, for, from, in, into, like, of, off, on, over, past, since, through, throughout, to, toward, under, underneath, until, up, upon, with, within,* and *without.*

Examples:

➡ In the cafeteria, students gathered to eat lunch.

➡ In the cafeteria at 11:00 A.M., students gathered to eat lunch.

➡ The child learned to read before his first birthday.

Skill #6

Write a Sentence with an Appositive Phrase
Appositives are phrases that rename a nearby noun or explain the noun more fully.

Examples:

➡ Mary, a creative cook, prepared her secret energy drink by placing a two-pound block of Spam into the blender and pouring in a gallon of buttermilk.

➡ Bill, a junior at Chief Sealth High School, likes to run every day after school.

➡ Every summer they travel to Morris Lake, a small lake in Minnesota.

Review of Sentence Skills *(cont.)*

Skill #7

Write a Sentence with a Participial Phrase
A participle is a verb that acts like an adjective to describe a noun.

Examples:

➡ Screaming loudly, the baseball fan celebrated his team's win.

➡ The children, covered in dirt, returned home from the camping trip.

➡ The team's star guard lost the game, missing a free throw.

Skill #8

Write a Sentence with a Predicate Noun
A predicate noun is a sentence in which a noun or pronoun is linked to another noun that renames, identifies, or explains the subject. Every predicate noun has a linking verb. Examples of *to be* linking verbs are *am, is, are, was, were, be, being,* and *been.* Other linking verbs include *appear, become, feel, grow, look, remain, seem, smell, sound,* and *taste.*

Examples:

➡ Time is money.

➡ Mary is a pastry chef.

➡ The new captain of the team will be Roberta.

Skill #9

Write a Sentence with a Predicate Adjective
In a predicate adjective, the subject of a sentence is linked with an adjective that describes the subject. See Skill #8 for a list of linking verbs.

Examples:

➡ Josh is tall and lean.

➡ The students seemed confused.

➡ Even in the daylight, the castle looked spooky.

Review of Sentence Skills *(cont.)*

Skill #10

Write a Complex Sentence with an Adverb Clause

A complex sentence is a sentence in which at least two ideas are combined into a single sentence. When an adverb clause is joined with a complete thought, it forms a complex sentence. Adverb clauses always begin with subordinating conjunctions. The following are examples of subordinating conjunctions:

Subordinating Conjunctions		
Time	**Cause and Effect**	**Contrast**
• after	• because	• although
• before	• since	• while
• as soon as	• if	• though
• as	• even though	• whereas
• when		• unless
• until		
• while		

Examples:

➡ When Bill went on vacation to Canada, he read 12 novels.

➡ Mary will major in English if she gets a scholarship and is able to attend college.

➡ Because he forgot his wedding anniversary for the tenth straight year, Roger spent a week sleeping on the porch.

Skill #11

Write a Complex Sentence with an Adjective Clause

A complex sentence is a sentence in which at least two ideas are combined into a single sentence. When an adjective clause is joined with a complete thought, it forms a complex sentence. Adjective clauses always begin with relative pronouns such as *who, whom, whose, which, that, when,* or *where.*

Examples:

➡ Bill, who loves to bowl, just bought a new ball.

➡ The family that lives down the street just bought a new car.

➡ Susan, who loves to swim in freezing water, recently joined the Polar Bear Club.

Review of Sentence Skills *(cont.)*

Skill #12

Write a Compound Sentence

When two complete ideas are joined using a coordinating conjunction, they form a compound sentence. Examples of coordinating conjunctions include *for, and, nor, but, or, yet,* and *so.*

Examples:

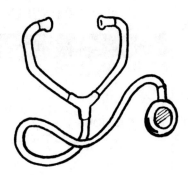

➡ Bill signed up for medical school, and he bought a new stethoscope.

➡ Jane read twelve novels last summer, but this summer she wants to read only magazines.

➡ Our neighborhood ice-cream man loves Elvis, and his ice-cream truck plays "Hound Dog."

Skill #13

Write a Compound-Complex Sentence

A compound-complex sentence combines at least three ideas into a single sentence. Compound-complex sentences feature at least two different kinds of connecting words that work to show the relationships between the ideas.

Set 1

Subordinating Conjunctions: after, before, as soon as, when, until, while, because, since, if, even though, although, while, though, whereas, unless

Relative Pronouns: who, whom, whose, which, that, when, or where

Set 2

Coordinating Conjunctions: for, and, nor, but, or, yet, so

Conjunctive Adverbs: also, as a result, consequently, for example, furthermore, however, moreover, otherwise, still, then, therefore, thus

Examples:

➡ Bill, who graduated from high school a year early, plans on going to college next year; therefore, he is planning on saving as much money as he can.

➡ After she ran five miles in the rain, Mary caught a bad cold, and she missed the next five days of school.

72

Review Quiz

Fill in the circle next to each correct answer.

1. **Which sentence has a compound subject?**

   (a) Until Russ learned to drive, he couldn't get to school on time for first period.

   (b) Russ loves to drive, but he hates to walk.

   (c) Russ and Mike always drive the speed limit.

   (d) Russ is a good driver, and he is also a good student.

2. **Which sentence has a compound predicate?**

   (a) After he ate lunch, the sophomore ran to class.

   (b) Jason and John ran to class to take their math test.

   (c) After eating lunch, the sophomore ran to class and took his math test.

   (d) Although he did not eat lunch, Jason did not feel hungry.

3. **Which sentence has a compound subject?**

   (a) If they win the lottery, John and Ann hope to quit their jobs.

   (b) If my candidate wins the election, I am hoping for a tax break.

   (c) In the city people move at a fast pace, but in the country people seem to slow down.

   (d) It seems to rain each time I try to wash my car.

4. **Which sentence contains adjectives?**

   (a) The quiet, stealthy cat crept up on the mouse.

   (b) The cat crept up on the mouse.

   (c) Quietly and stealthily, the cat crept up on the mouse.

   (d) The cat crept up on the mouse.

5. **Which sentence contains adjectives?**

   (a) The student started his homework early.

   (b) The summer school students read their books quietly.

   (c) Opening their books to read, the students smiled in anticipation.

   (d) Eagerly, the student started his homework early.

6. **Which sentence opens with an adverb?**

   (a) The running back ran swiftly through the defense.

   (b) The swift running back ran through the defense.

   (c) Swiftly, the running back ran through the defense.

   (d) Swift and strong, the running back ran through the defense.

Review Quiz *(cont.)*

Fill in the circle next to each correct answer.

7. Which sentence has at least one prepositional phrase?

(a) I like bowling.

(b) Joe, Ron, and Ray are postal workers.

(c) Math is fun, but I enjoy art class more.

(d) The children always come running when the ice-cream truck drives through our neighborhood.

8. Which sentence contains an appositive phrase?

(a) Joe, the best writer in his class, is an outstanding juggler.

(b) Joe, who loves to juggle, is the best writer in his class.

(c) Joe loves to juggle, and he is the best writer in his class.

(d) Joe loves to juggle; in addition, he is the best writer in his class.

9. Which of the following sentences contains a participial phrase?

(a) Larry, singing loudly in the shower, forgot the words to "Dancing Queen."

(b) Mara loves to sing and dance as she completes her geometry homework.

(c) Singing and dancing are Emily's favorite hobbies.

(d) He never sang, but he loved to dance.

10. Which of the following has a predicate noun?

(a) Ron, a freshman at Walla Walla High School, is never unhappy.

(b) Ron is a freshman at Walla Walla High School.

(c) Ron, who is a freshman at Walla Walla High School, is never unhappy.

(d) Ron is happy.

11. Which of the following has a predicate adjective?

(a) The demanding customer would not take "no" for an answer.

(b) His new computer does not have a word processing program.

(c) The broken guitar stood quietly against the wall.

(d) Larry is talkative.

12. Which of the following sentences contains an adverb clause?

(a) After lunch, John read a novel, walked his dog, and cleaned his garage.

(b) John cleaned his garage after he ate lunch.

(c) After dinner, John cleaned his garage, and he also walked his dog.

(d) John read a long novel after lunch, but he forgot to clean the garage.

Review Quiz *(cont.)*

Fill in the circle next to each correct answer.

13. Which of the following sentences contains an adjective clause?

(a) Susan loves to swim in freezing water.

(b) Susan loves to swim in freezing water even if she has to break the ice on the lake first.

(c) Susan, who loves to swim in freezing water, never gets colds.

(d) After swimming for hours in freezing water, Susan takes a dip in the hot tub.

14. Which of the following is a compound sentence?

(a) After she finished playing the piano, Sara nervously sang a soft, sweet love song.

(b) Sara played the piano and sang a soft, sweet song.

(c) Nervously, Sara played the piano, and she sang a soft, sweet song.

(d) Playing the piano and singing a sweet love song, Sara was nervous.

15. Which of the following is a compound sentence?

(a) As Carl takes his calculus test, he sweats profusely.

(b) Carl is taking a calculus test and is doing poorly.

(c) Biting his pencil, Carl is taking a calculus test.

(d) Carl is taking a calculus test, and he is doing poorly on it.

16. Which of the following is a compound sentence?

(a) Joe is talking to a girl on the phone, but his mind is somewhere else.

(b) As Joe talks to a girl on the phone, his mind is somewhere else.

(c) Joe is talking to a girl on the phone while his mind is somewhere else.

(d) Joe, who is talking to a girl on the phone, is thinking about something else.

17. Which of the following is a compound-complex sentence?

(a) Blake bought a new guitar and hopes to be in a famous band someday.

(b) After Blake buys his new guitar, he hopes to be in a famous band.

(c) Although Blake does not like to practice and does not really like music, he hopes to be in a famous band someday.

(d) After Blake buys a new guitar, he plans to join a band, and he hopes to be famous someday.

18. Which of the following is a compound-complex sentence?

(a) Eric is frequently late for work, but he always leaves work on time.

(b) Because his alarm clock is broken, Eric is frequently late for work; however, he always leaves work right on time.

(c) Because his alarm clock is broken, Eric is frequently late for work.

(d) Eric is frequently late for work.

Using the Sentence Skills in Combination

Any two of the sentence skills listed below may be combined in a single sentence:

1. Write a Sentence with a Compound Subject or Compound Predicate

2. Write a Sentence with Adjectives

3. Write a Sentence with Adverbs

4. Write a Sentence with a Prepositional Phrase

5. Write a Sentence with an Appositive Phrase

6. Write a Sentence with a Participial Phrase

7. Write a Sentence with a Predicate Noun or Predicate Adjective

8. Write a Complex Sentence with an Adverb Clause

9. Write a Complex Sentence with an Adjective Clause

10. Write a Compound–Complex Sentence

Using this list of sentence skills and combining any two into a single sentence, there are almost 100 different possible combinations. When combined with the 40 topics on pages 65–67, there are nearly 4,000 possible writing assignments.

Here are some examples of single-sentence writing assignments that a teacher might assign using different combinations of sentence skills and topics.

Sample Single-Sentence Writing Assignments

→ Write a complex sentence with an adverb clause and an appositive phrase on topic #4 from page 65.

→ Write a compound-complex sentence with a predicate noun or adjective on topic #20 from page 66.

→ Write a complex sentence with an adjective clause and adjectives on topic #27 from page 66.

→ Write a sentence with a prepositional phrase and a participial phrase on topic #8 from page 65.

→ Write a complex sentence with an adverb clause and a prepositional phrase on topic #34 from page 67.

Using the Sentence Skills in Combination *(cont.)*

Here are some examples of possible combinations that could be made on topic #21 (page 66): Write the opening sentence of a short story about a character in conflict with himself/herself. Think about a difficult decision or complex problem the character must solve.

1. Sentence with Adjectives and an Adverb:

➡ Ron Bailey, thoughtful and intelligent, spent all afternoon quietly thinking about a plan to end his string of bad luck.

2. Sentence with a Prepositional Phrase and a Participial Phrase:

➡ Sitting in his bedroom all day, Ron Bailey sat thinking quietly about a plan to end his long string of bad luck.

3. Compound-Complex Sentence with a Predicate Adjective or Predicate Noun:

➡ Ron Bailey is a young man who is searching for a plan to end his long string of bad luck, and he knows that he needs to come up with a plan before it is too late.

4. Sentence with a Predicate Adjective or Predicate Noun and a Prepositional Phrase:

➡ Ron Bailey is a serious young man searching for a plan to end his long string of bad luck.

5. Complex Sentence with an Adjective Clause and an Appositive Phrase:

➡ Ron Bailey, a serious, thoughtful young man, sat thinking about a plan that would end his long string of bad luck.

6. Sentence with a Participial Phrase and an Appositive Phrase:

➡ Straining his brain, Ron Bailey, a serious young man, tried to think of an idea to end his long string of bad luck.

Answer Key

Page 7

1. Ben, copied
2. readers, enjoy
3. squirrels, hibernate
4. dogs, ran
5. we, plan
6. *Star Wars,* is
7. Jack, does
8. madman, walked

Pages 10 and 11

1. Subject: Ben
   Predicates: copied, turned
   compound predicate
2. Subjects: readers, subscribers
   Predicate: enjoy
   compound subject
3. Subjects: Jeff, Val
   Predicates: spent
   compound subject
4. Subject: dogs
   Predicates: barked, ran
   compound predicate
5. Subjects: freshmen, sophmores
   Predicate: plan
   compound subject
6. Subjects: *Titanic, Star Wars*
   Predicate: are
   compound subject
7. Subject: Fred
   Predicates: sang, wrote, read
   compound predicate
8. Subjects: Jack, Ron
   Predicate: do
   compound subject

Sentence Combining: Answers may vary; possible answers listed below.

1. Last Saturday, Ron mowed his lawn, watched eight straight hours of golf, and rearranged his refrigerator-magnet collection.
2. The books, magazines, and newspapers were stacked all over the room.
3. Boris woke up at 5:00 A.M., jumped out of bed, and began doing one-arm push-ups.

Pages 14 and 15

1. loud, annoying, ice cream
2. restless, eager
3. new, electric, accordion
4. high-pressure, water
5. electric, car
6. mysterious, unexplained, doghouse
7. first, electric, washboard
8. cold, freezing

Sentence Combining: Answers may vary; possible answers listed below.

1. Their peaceful, relaxing evening was interrupted by a barrage of calls by an annoying phone solicitor.
2. Joe built a 500-foot tower out of empty milk cartons.
3. Marsha's favorite meal is eggplant smothered in hot maple syrup.

Pages 18 and 19

1. greedily
2. none
3. guiltily
4. politely
5. profusely
6. quietly
7. loudly, clearly
8. gingerly

Sentence Combining: Answers may vary; possible answers listed below.

1. Mary's head swayed rhythmically as she listened to her favorite CD.
2. Bill anxiously opened his letter from the Long Ranger Fan Club.
3. Quickly and quietly, Nancy slipped her overdue library books into the return slot.

Page 23

1. (in) his sweaty bowling shoes
2. (in) his shower, (on) his lawn
3. (with) big blue eyes, (into) his bank account
4. (in) a loud, raspy voice
5. (before) his first birthday
6. (in) the city sewer system
7. (Over) the mountain, (through) the forest, (for) five hours, (before) they stopped to ask, (for) directions
8. (in) a dirty T-shirt, (under) the house

Answer Key *(cont.)*

Sentence Combining: Answers may vary; possible answers listed below.

1. In her neon pink swimsuit, Susan swam towards the shore.
2. The books on the library bookshelf were out-of-date encyclopedias.
3. Bill kept his prize-winning photographs of mailboxes in a leather-bound photo album.

Pages 26 and 27

Nouns	Appositives
1. men	old friends
2. Ron Smith	the world's most honest police officer
3. 1968	145 years later
4. song	an old Scottish waltz
5. speech	the shortest in history
6. cat	a large tabby
7. Joy	an avid photographer
8. Ron	a miler on our high school track team

Sentence Combining: Answers may vary; possible answers listed below.

1. Felix took his two most valuable possessions, his baseball cards and his pet slug, with him on his vacation.
2. Callie, an amateur ventriloquist, wants to teach her dummy how to speak French.
3. Joe sat quietly eating his favorite meal, a cottage cheese and Spam sandwich.

Pages 30 and 31

1. Reading a magazine article on effective flossing techniques
2. laughing at the joke
3. Eating a banana, eating an ice-cream cone
4. Guzzling a half-gallon of past-date 2% milk in 60 seconds
5. repairing the chili pump at the corner convenience store
6. Using a separate car key for each of his ears
7. Spending at least four hours brainstorming
8. Removing a large glob of gum from his mouth
9. Taking copious notes on the differences between males and females

Sentence Combining: Answers may vary; possible answers listed below.

1. Hoping to find his missing sweat sock, Gary plunged his arm into the dirty-clothes hamper.
2. Linda, singing every Beatles song she knew, tried to entertain her guests from England.
3. Talking in a loud, raspy voice, the woman annoyed everyone by giving away the movie's ending.

Page 34

1. PN, is
2. PN, is
3. X
4. PN, will be
5. X
6. PN, is
7. PN, are
8. PN, is

Page 38

1. PA, is
2. PA, were
3. PA, is
4. PA, is
5. X
6. PA, are
7. PA, is
8. X

Page 43

1. (Although) he was tired, mad, and hungry
2. None
3. (even though) he does not have a job
4. (When) he found out that the price for the buffet did not include a soft drink
5. (When) Luke made homemade ice cream
6. (Since) there are 85 billion different possibilities for the first four moves of a chess game
7. (If) you add kiwi fruit to gelatin
8. (When) he began using his phone book to call random numbers

Sentence Combining: Answers may vary; possible answers listed below.

1. Even though he spent all night working on it, Pedro was unable to finish his project, a solar-powered toothbrush.
2. After Ron finds a cure for the common cold and for hiccups, he wants to retire and live in Florida.
3. When the teacher announced that the test was cancelled, the class cheered.

Answer Key *(cont.)*

Page 47

1. who is a big Alfred Hitchcock fan
2. who had spent too many nights sleeping next to his horse
3. which we bought as a present for our parents' anniversary
4. none
5. who loves to bowl, who loves to eat chili
6. who was not very smart
7. which was 30 feet long
8. which was hidden for 17 centuries

Sentence Combining: Answers may vary; possible answers listed below.

1. In 1940, a tornado that uncovered buried gold showered gold coins over a Russian town.
2. Joe enjoys novels that feature fearless, adventurous characters.
3. The mayor, who did not want to get re-elected, proposed an ordinance against polka dancing.

Page 50

1. Y, but
2. N
3. Y, but
4. Y, but
5. Y, but
6. N
7. Y, so
8. Y, and

Sentence Combining: Answers may vary; possible answers listed below.

1. Sheila spent three hours writing her essay, but she didn't spend any time proofreading it.
2. Our computer is not working, so don't send us any e-mail.
3. In the morning Ron always sings Irish ballads, and in the evening he always sings patriotic hymns.

Page 53

	Set 1	Set 2
1.	which, when	
2.	that, because	and
3.	when	however
4.	when, that	therefore
5.	when	as a result

Sentence Combining: Answers may vary; possible answers listed below.

1. Although his car runs, the air conditioning is broken, and his 8-track tape player plays only in reverse.
2. The substitute teacher, who was having a rough day, forgot to assign the homework, so the class had twice as much homework the following night.
3. Since your computer continues to break down, you should have the hard drive repaired, or you should buy a new computer.

Page 62

Counterfeit Sentence Game: Sentence #2 is the actual sentence.

Pages 73–75

1. c
2. c
3. a
4. a
5. b
6. c
7. d
8. a
9. a
10. b
11. d
12. b
13. c
14. c
15. d
16. a
17. d
18. b